HANDBOOKS FOR RESEARCH IN POLITICAL BEHAVIOR

edited by James A. Robinson

CONTENT ANALYSIS

content analysis

A HANDBOOK WITH APPLICATIONS
FOR THE STUDY
OF INTERNATIONAL CRISIS

ROBERT C. NORTH   •   OLE R. HOLSTI
M. GEORGE ZANINOVICH   •   DINA A. ZINNES

NORTHWESTERN UNIVERSITY PRESS   1963

EDITOR'S FOREWORD

This book will introduce the general social scientist to "content analysis" as a technique for systematic research among documents which record written or oral messages. It will also be of interest to the specialized student for its discussion of the use of content analysis in the original researches of Robert C. North and his colleagues on the origins of World War I and on contemporary Sino-Soviet relations. Because the presentation of the technique is embedded in the substance of the authors' work, readers will readily find concrete illustrations of method, plus theoretical guides for deciding whether, when, and what form of content analysis should be used. Scholars, who argue that method and substance are integrally related and should not be separated for purposes of instruction, will be pleased by the way in which the authors have prefaced their presentation of different kinds of content analysis with an introduction to the concepts and theoretical assumptions used in their studies of international crisis. At the same time, students who wish to borrow from the assorted versions of content analysis will hopefully find that the illustrations from international crises help them to understand the techniques without confinement to the subject of crisis.

The special forms of content analysis discussed in Part II of this manual are the conventional frequency count and qualitative identifications (Chapter III), Q-Sort (Chapter IV), pair-comparisons (Chapter V), and evaluative assertion analysis (Chapter VI). Conventional identifications of qualitative characteristics of content and counts of their appearance are valuable for accurate and operational summaries of documents. Such applications of content analysis are relatively simple, quickly learnable, and relevant to almost any social science. The historian John

A. Garraty has indicated how these devices may practicably be used in history and biography.[1]

The Q-Sort is less elementary, will require closer study, and for under-graduates will probably involve the instructor more directly in learning its use. The purpose of this variation of content analysis is to measure the *intensity* of attitudinal and behavioral characteristics of decision-makers and not merely to *identify* or count them. The statistics introduced are elementary, however; the formulae may be worked if the student has learned algebra. The Q-Sort is limited to certain kinds of data, as explained in Section II of Chapter IV. When the assumptions for the use of Q-Sort do not hold, alternative scaling techniques such as "pair-comparisons" may be available, as described in Chapter V.

Evaluative assertion analysis, another variant of content analytic tools, is applicable to any dimension defined as a continuum between polar opposites, such as strong-weak, like-dislike, decisive-indecisive, violent-non-violent. It is perhaps still more complicated than Q-Sort and pair-comparisons, but the reader who follows the progression of the chapters will find the description of the technique sufficient to introduce him to more technical usages referred to in the footnotes to Chapter VI.

The authors go beyond the presentation of these descriptive techniques of coding, categorizing, and characterizing data. In Part III they introduce ways of organizing and synthesizing data derived from content analysis. At this point they summarize essential features of "functional distance analysis" and "factor analysis" with special reference to models of international conflict (Chapter VII). In addition, the concluding chapter indicates potential conjunctions of high-speed digital computers with content analytic techniques. Political scientists have been somewhat slower than their colleagues in other political behavior-related disciplines to capitalize on the time-saving and creative advantages of machine processing of data. However, the appearance of such manuals as this, plus the gradual increase in mathematical training in political science, foreshadow the day when the mistrust, misunderstanding, and mystery associated with such devices will pass.

One point which this volume cogently stresses is the necessity of replicable, operational techniques in testing theoretically derived hypotheses. Political science and political sociology have well-earned reputations for researching "big" and "important" problems. However difficult it may be to distinguish trivial from important problems, no one seriously wishes political science to depart from its central problems, those which have been the subject of the discipline from Aristotle to the present. At the same time, political science has had a poor reputation for empirical skills devoted to testing hypotheses systematically. The pioneer studies of voting emerged among sociologists. Virtually the first scientific attitudinal study, although it appeared in the *American Political Science Review*, was by non-political scientists.[2] The technical innovations of the 1920's, pioneered by Merriam, Rice, Gosnell, Lasswell, and others of "the Chicago school," were a generation in coming to acceptance, and by then sociology and psychology were technically more complicated (if not more sophisticated) fields of study.

But political science is certain to add technical sophistication to its arsenal. Then, and only then, can it discriminatingly validate its plethora of great ideas and separate the attractive hypothetical speculation from the confirmed, evidence-supported proposition. This series and this volume are meant as modest contributions toward training specialists to hasten that era and to instruct generalists who—as citizens, governmental policy-makers, and educational administrators—will appreciate the trend and underwrite its progress.

The authors note that techniques of the kind described in this book often require group activity and teamwork. This is so because of the immensely detailed and multi-faceted character of the research. The lone scholar cannot always undertake all the minute aspects of a large research problem; time and the range of skills required are more than a single worker possesses. Nevertheless, the size of problems remains and can not be reduced; resources must simply be increased. This manual will help course- and seminar-related projects to differentiate tasks in a practicable and solution-oriented way. Other sciences, including the medical, biological, and physical sciences, have learned to increase resources by combining individual specialized efforts.[3]

Professor North and his colleagues represent such an attempt in political science. The integration reflected in this handbook illustrates the kind of co-ordination the use of refined research techniques requires.

A few more general points about the series are in order. This is a series of research handbooks for undergraduates to use with instruction, and graduate students and post-doctoral researchers to use without instruction. The object is to cover, eventually, several research methods of interest to political science and political sociology. The initial volumes also include introduction to field surveys, statistics, data processing techniques and equipment, and gross electoral data analysis. Further volumes are expected to include techniques as diverse as legislative roll call methods and participant-observation.

Publication of the series is based on the conviction that the recent empirical emphasis in the study of political behavior ought to be encouraged, and that adequate instructional materials for the use of empirical techniques are not readily available, except in highly technical form usually illustrated by non-political data. This is not meant to disparage the scholarly and scientific treatises which have established the validity of various research techniques. Indeed, one of the aims of each volume is to introduce the reader to this advanced and technical literature. However, in addition to the basic, extant works, there is an evident need for introductory, elementary, yet sound, materials which undergraduates, graduates, and their faculties can master in a relatively short period of time and apply during courses covering central topics of empirical political theory.

Since the end of World War II, considerable emphasis has been put on undergraduates having direct contact with the real world of politics and public affairs. The founding of the Citizenship Clearing House in 1946 and the diffusion of affiliate organizations in nearly half the states have contributed substantially to this development. Other sources give impetus by putting students "into the field" to participate in political campaigns, conduct public opinion polls, observe city councils and state legislatures, and to "intern" in offices of Congressmen. In 1953 the American Political Science Association began a program of one-year fellowships for post-doctoral political scientists and young journalists to work in House and Senate offices. Hundreds of less substantial Washington internships have developed, until in 1962 the APSA and the National Center for Education in Politics (formerly Citizenship Clearing House) established a co-ordinator in Washington to bring some order to the programs and restore the original educational emphasis.

Meanwhile college enrollments continue to increase, which further adds to the teaching requirements of liberal arts colleges and universities. Simultaneously political science professionalization is increasing. Many young political scientists experience tension between their college teaching expectations and their professional research goals acquired in graduate schools. Some find a compromise between these cross-pressures by involving their undergraduates in research. A number of substantial reasons commend this development to professors, students, and administrators. For one thing, it is an obvious and compelling way to teach something about procedures of knowledge acquisition, as distinguished from what passes for current findings. As growth in knowledge radically increases, methods are likely to be less perishable than particular factual "conclusions." For another, it follows a classical learning principle—providing individually-paced instruction with opportunity for intimate faculty-student collaboration which promptly feeds back reinforcement for research which meets required standards. For still another, the improving quality of undergraduates throughout American colleges means that students are increasingly apt to possess the necessary intellectual and creative talents to do what was not expected of the previous generation of college students—i.e., to discover new knowledge as well as to acquire old.

The fulfillment of these hopes has, however, been held up by the frequent lack of knowledge of research skills. Political science departments have been slow to follow sociology and psychology with research methods courses of their own. As a result, the field-oriented courses, such as political parties and elections, public opinion, legislative process, and public administration, have remained handicapped. Empirically-oriented courses such as foreign policy-making, international relations, and political behavior have also remained handicapped. Academic semesters and quarters simply have not been long enough to do all that is conventionally required and at the same time to teach basic research skills in sampling, interviewing, coding, analysis, etc. Especially has this been the case in the absence of reasonably concise yet authoritative handbooks for the most frequently used techniques. This has been true for graduate training as well as undergraduate education.

Therefore, this series was conceived to provide what was not available. For impetus in planning the series I am indebted to Evron M. Kirkpatrick, Harold D. Lasswell, and Howard Penniman. At the first regional seminar on Political Science in the Sixties held at Madison, Wisconsin, in June, 1960, we discussed and deplored the absence of materials such as this series aims to supply. Further conversations with Richard C. Snyder led to the suggestion that the Northwestern University Press might publish these volumes. It is the hope of all who have been associated with these handbooks that they will serve to bury the hatchet between "teachers" and "researchers" and help to restore the classical conception of a university to students of political activity—i.e., that learning is the transmission *and* acquisition of knowledge acquired by others *and* by oneself, that there can be no *research* without the organized and continuing *search* and that in being outdated by new technical developments they prove again that to discover new knowledge is to repeal much of the old.

JAMES A. ROBINSON

NOTES

[1] *The Nature of Biography* (New York: Alfred A. Knopf, Inc., 1957), pp. 223-37; and "The Application of Content Analysis to Biography and History," in Ithiel de Sola Pool (ed.), *Trends in Content Analysis* (Urbana: University of Illinois Press, 1959), pp. 171-88.

[2] F. H. Allport and D. A. Hartman, "The Measurement and Motivation of an Atypical Opinion in a Certain Group," *American Political Science Review*, 19 (1925), 735-60.

[3] For a study of group work in building a distinguished medical institution for both research and teaching, *see* Helen Clappesattle, *The Doctors Mayo* (Minneapolis: University of Minnesota Press, 1941), esp. Chapters 18-22.

PREFACE

This handbook represents an attempt to challenge the traditional and widespread contention that decisions affecting international relations, and especially those decisions made by "irresponsible decision-makers," are "too enigmatic to be analyzed at all" and that leaps must therefore be made into the dark. It questions beliefs and sentiments such as that expressed by Harold Macmillan in a foreign affairs debate in the House of Commons in 1955—a statement which a former U.S. Secretary of State endorsed in a discussion at Stanford in 1962—that the foreign policy moves of a state—and particularly the moves of states such as the Soviet Union—can be interpreted "either as reassuring signs of a new policy" or as "sinister warnings of a more subtle, but just as deadly threat." How, then, should they be assessed? "One can speculate on that forever . . . what we have to do is act."

The several authors of this handbook believe that decisions affecting international relations can not only be analyzed but that perhaps there are conditions, trends, rules, developments, laws, inner consistencies, attachments, orders, systems, and principles which do affect decisions and decision-makers, and that these can be sought, discovered, sorted, compared, analyzed, and assessed. Projected against the record of history which offers a wealth of information on the way decisions were made and how decision-makers have fashioned policies in the past, these factors are bound to be helpful in the assessment of the chief attributes of the intellectual processes of decision-makers responsible for policy. And if assisted in their labors by modern mechanical tools, facilities, and instruments—of which the computers are perhaps the most important—who knows; perhaps the "leaps into dark" may be postponed or possibly even eliminated in the future.

This handbook, like the studies from which it emerged, is truly a group undertaking. Among the contributors are literally dozens of individuals whose participation has been crucial: students who coded materials from a variety of languages; scalers who bore with us through many months of experimentation and contributed important suggestions; and advisors from many disciplines at Stanford, from various other universities and colleges, and from government. In particular, we are indebted to Mrs. Helen Grace whose patience, skills, knowledge of channels, and devotion have proved invaluable throughout this undertaking. We gratefully acknowledge the aid and assistance of all these people for making the handbook possible. For inadequacies, oversights, aberrations, and errors, on the other hand, solely we are responsible.

Stanford, September 18, 1962

O.R.H.
R.C.N.
D.Z.
M.G.Z.

CONTENTS

Editor's Foreword ix

Preface xv

Introduction xvii

PART I: FRAME OF REFERENCE

Chapter I. Purpose, Definitions, and Basic Assumptions 3

PART II: DATA PREPARATION

Chapter II. Documents as a Source of Data 17

Chapter III. The Quantitative Analysis of Content 37

Chapter IV. Measuring Intensity of Attitudes and Behavior 55

Chapter V. "Pair Comparison" Scaling in International Relations 79

Chapter VI. Evaluative Assertion Analysis 91

PART III: MODES OF ANALYSIS

Chapter VII. Pattern Analysis and Factor Analysis 105

Chapter VIII. Computer Content Analysis 131

Appendix A: Propositions about the Behavior of States in the International System 149

Appendix B: Propositions from the 1914 Crisis 161

Bibliography 179

(notes follow at end of chapters)

INTRODUCTION

The concepts, contents, methods, sources, and results contained in this handbook have emerged from a comparative study of historical crises undertaken by the Studies in International Conflict and Integration at Stanford University.

In February, 1960, the Ford Foundation awarded Stanford University funds to enlarge the research and teaching program in the processes of international conflict and integration. Already under way on an exploratory basis, this project had been applying techniques from several disciplines to the study of international relations. As developed since that time, the studies in International Conflict and Integration have become a systematic inquiry into the nature, processes, and effects of conflict and integration in transactions between nation states.

Actually, the enterprise began in the autumn of 1957 with a small voluntary inter-disciplinary seminar of the Stanford University faculty interested in international relations. The faculty met twice a month to consider how problems of international relations could be formulated and analyzed with greater insight, precision, and result. Underlying faculty discontent with prevailing approaches to international relations was the sober realization that successes in the physical sciences and technology had far outstripped our knowledge of human behavior and our control of human conflicts—especially on the world level. Among the fifteen or twenty persons who met each fortnight were men and women from political science, history, economics, psychology, sociology, anthropology, education, law, physics, and electronics. From the beginning there was notable consensus about the magnitude of the challenge and the inadequacies of tools at hand. There was much less agreement on what should be done.

With successive meetings the seminar itself became increasingly an arena of "conflict".

As discussions progressed, it became evident that two different tendencies were emerging. There were those who considered the conflictual processes in human affairs to be the crucial factor; and there were others who felt that we should begin by investigating the similarities, rather than the differences, the areas of cohesion and consensus rather than the dissensions, the processes of integration, rather than those of conflict.

By year's end it was decided to start with a conflict situation— the European crisis of 1914—and subject it to exhaustive investigation and analysis. Subsequently, as this undertaking progressed, it became evident that the cleavage between the two view points was not as devastating as some of us had felt. For even in the peak of crisis we found the conflictual and integrative processes almost inextricably intertwined. By starting with conflict, we soon found ourselves conceptualizing integration, and surely if we had begun with integration we would have been forced into an analysis of conflict.

One consequence of the faculty discussions and of early investigations into the 1914 crisis was a paper by Wilbur Schramm and Robert C. North, "International Relations as a Behavior System." This study provided central hypotheses and a partial, somewhat tentative background theory for subsequent studies of the 1914 and other crises. Inevitably the joint effort represented in this paper has had a strong influence in shaping both the empirical research and the basic model presented in the present handbook.

Partly as an outgrowth of the 1914 investigations Project Michelson of the Naval Ordnance Test Station (NOTS), China Lake, California awarded the Studies in International Conflict and Integration a small contract to apply similar techniques in an analysis of the Sino-Soviet controversy. Subsequently, a short-term, follow-up contract was awarded to evaluate, refine, and extend the methodology that had been developed. And after that a further contract was awarded to adapt the General Inquirer System for Content Analysis by IBM 7090 computer, as developed by Philip Stone and his associates, to problems of international politics.

In conjunction with these and related contracts in other universities, NOTS arranged with the Center for Advanced Study in the Behavioral Sciences at Stanford to bring together during the summer of 1962 a small work group consisting of Thomas Milburn (Project Michelson); Robert C. North (Studies in International Conflict and Integration, Stanford University); Charles E. Osgood (Institute of Communication Research, University of Illinois); Ithiel de Sola Pool (Department of Political Science, Massachusetts Institute of Technology); Wilbur Schramm (Institute of Communication Research, Stanford University); and Richard C. Snyder (International Relations Program, Northwestern University). The major purpose was to consider problems of command and control and of deterrence within the larger context of international affairs in a nuclear age, but considerable emphasis was placed upon an examination of basic assumptions, conceptualization, and research techniques.

As an outgrowth of the summer's preoccupation Charles E. Osgood and Robert C. North undertook the task of considering the feasibility of a rigorous theory of behavior which would encompass the individual, the group, and the nation state. This investigation is still in progress at this writing, but inevitably the group discussions associated with the undertaking have influenced several portions of this handbook.

The handbook consists of three parts: Part I, which serves as a frame of reference and general introduction to the whole undertaking, is essentially a normative construct for the study of states in crisis, and is supplemented by Appendix A and Appendix B. Part II embodies coding and scaling techniques applicable to theory developed in Part I. And Part III contains examples of the different kinds of analysis that can be done with the data provided by Part II. The two appendices illustrate propositions which are being tested with the techniques.

In particular, *Robert C. North* describes in Part I and in the appendices some relationships between individual and state behavior, puts forward a model for the study of states in crises, and derives from the 1914 conflict a series of propositions for further study. *Dina Zinnes* in her two chapters surveys and describes ways of selecting and preparing historical documents for quantitative analysis and alternate techniques of scaling intensities. *Ole R. Holsti* examines stages in content analysis research and defines and illustrates categories dealing with perception of cognitive and affective matters. In his chapter on evaluative assertion analysis, Holsti discusses an alternative technique of coding, scaling, and analyzing written text; in his chapter on computer analysis, he introduces and elaborates upon the feasibility of turning over many of the research tasks described in Part II to computers. *M. George Zaninovich,* in the first of his two chapters, describes ways of scaling intensities of hostility, frustration, and other variables; in his second chapter, he discusses ways of analyzing trends and patterns in the behavior of these variables, and suggests two generic models of crisis.

This handbook is, in a sense, also a progress report, a report on progress of research conducted by the Studies in International Conflict and Integration at Stanford University. We had a good start, but much remains to be done. This is why we wish to invite suggestions, criticism, and comments which the users of the handbook may note in the course of their study of this volume. We will welcome any assistance and co-operation which would bring us closer to our goal.

Stanford, September 18, 1962

JAN F. TRISKA

PART I: FRAME OF REFERENCE

CHAPTER I* PURPOSE, DEFINITIONS, AND BASIC ASSUMPTIONS

Purpose

The purpose of this handbook is to introduce the reader to the use of content analysis with illustrations from new ways of studying international crises and the behavior of states in conflict.[1] †We assume that the systematic and comparative investigation of crisis situations in history will provide clues to the paths that lead into war, and will also suggest alternatives to large scale violence as a mode of conflict. It is only by the comparative investigation of many different cases that it will become feasible to develop a theory of international behavior which can be used with rigor and confidence.

With these ends in view we have divided this handbook into three parts.

The first part together with the appendices presents a number of general propositions about human behavior; some possible relationships between the individual—both as a citizen and as a leader—and the national system of which he is a part; a model of state behavior under various circumstances including those of crisis; and a derivation—from the European crisis of 1914[2]—of basic propositions about international behavior for further testing.

The second part of the handbook provides content analytic techniques for reduction of crisis transactions into basic units and for determining their variation in terms of intensity. Problems relating to sources and historical documentation as well

---

* The major author of Part I is Robert C. North, who has drawn heavily upon personal discussions with Charles E. Osgood and also upon Osgood's published writings and unpublished work papers.

†Notes will be found at the end of each chapter.

as a system for defining categories and coding basic recording units, are discussed first. Then a set of techniques for measuring the intensity of expression for selected variables is presented. Part II provides the tools which will serve to test the hypotheses submitted in the appendices.

The third part suggests ways in which the data from historical crises can be analyzed and further tests constructed. It also discusses the adaptation of computer technology to content analysis of sources relating to international transactions. This part of the handbook has special relevance for the problem of a day-to-day analysis and interpretation of the behavior of states.

The Dimensions of Crisis

The word *crisis* comes from the Greek *krinein,* to separate. In traditional medical terms a crisis denotes that change in a disease which indicates whether the outcome is to be recovery or death.[3] Broadly, the crisis refers to that point of time when it is decided whether an affair or course of action will go on or be modified or reach a termination point.

In pneumonia the crisis is brought about when *pneumococci*—usually in collaboration with some minor infection of the respiratory tract—threaten to overwhelm the antibodies which function with other bodily processes as a coping mechanism for preservation of the system. The crisis may be identified as that period of time when the struggle between the *pneumococci* and antibodies is in grave doubt.

The usual indicators of crisis in a disease are physical symptoms such as heart action, blood pressure, respiration, body temperature, and the like. In general, the symptoms are consequences of the struggle between the antecedent agents—*pneumococci* and antibodies—and are not causal to the crisis. It must be noted at the same time, however, that a symptom—such as an extreme rise of bodily temperature—may function as an intervening variable which appears to determine—or at least to affect strongly—the outcome of the crisis.

The antecedent agents of an international crisis are seldom easy to isolate. In general, we might identify them as the issues in conflict which the normal coping mechanisms of the society find difficult to accommodate. As with many physical diseases, we assume that they tend to be present in the international system— in one form or another and to one degree or another—at all times. A crisis comes about when there is a weakening of the coping mechanisms to a point where the issues in conflict tend to overwhelm them; or when new issues arise for which the coping mechanisms are not adequate.

Among typical coping mechanisms in the international system we might include international law and custom; diplomacy, treaties, and various channels of negotiation and interchange; public international unions and institutions of international arbitration, and adjudication such as the United Nations; and so forth.

Levels of Analysis

We find it useful to define the state as a *system,* that is, a boundary-maintaining set of inter-dependent particles or sub-units—and also as an actor in a larger, international system. In similar terms, the state may be viewed as occupying one level in a multi-level hierarchy of systems. By *interdependence* we mean that whatever happens to one component of a system affects, no matter how slightly, the balance and relationships of the whole system. By boundary, we mean that the components are so related that it is possible to ascertain where the system ends and the environment begins.

As we proceed it will become evident how the state, while functioning as a system in one context, can be viewed also as a component of the wider, international system. Whether a given unit is viewed as a system then, or an actor, or a component within a larger, encompassing system, depends upon the perspective appropriate to the analysis at hand.

Each system, at any level, must be susceptible to analysis into a set of systems at the next subordinate level. It is assumed here, moreover, that the minimum necessary and sufficient processes displayed by the supraordinate system will be displayed by the subordinate systems—at their own level of functioning—and vice versa.

LEVELS   OF   SYSTEMS

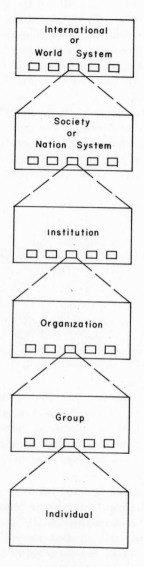

FIGURE I-1

Let us suppose that on one system level an organization receives, transmits, and interprets incoming information, and then makes decisions and transmits and executes them. According to basic assumption, any subordinate *group* within the organization—such as the information transmitting group—will also receive, transmit, and interpret *its* information and then make decisions and transmit and execute them. The group, in turn, should be exhaustively analysable into *individual* sub-systems, each sub-system displaying information and decision processing functions that are functionally analogous.

These necessary and sufficient processes should be found functionally equivalent at all levels of analysis. Under this assumption we would expect that principles found to be operating on any one level would be transferable to the functionally equivalent processes at other levels.

Within this conceptual framework the world—or, for our purposes, the international community—functions as the most supra-ordinate system; and the various nation states are its sub-systems. On the next subordinate level are institutions: political, economic, religious, communication, and so forth. Each institution is composed of organizations; each organization encompasses groups; and each group is comprised of individuals.

Figure I-1 suggests six distinguishable system levels that seem useful for this conceptualization.

Specialized functions

A system, at any level, may be characterized as having some degree of organization, that is, some degree of specialization in function of its sub-systems. We postulate that the greater the degree of organization on each system level, the stronger will be the tendency toward analogy of function up and down the hierarchy.

In highly oversimplified fashion we have used Figure I-2 as a means of suggesting those functions which seem minimal and sufficient for various system levels, that is, translation, projection, integration, and the central decision-making functions.

By *translation* we mean the total processes whereby, on the one hand, data from the environment are translated into a form

FIGURE I-2

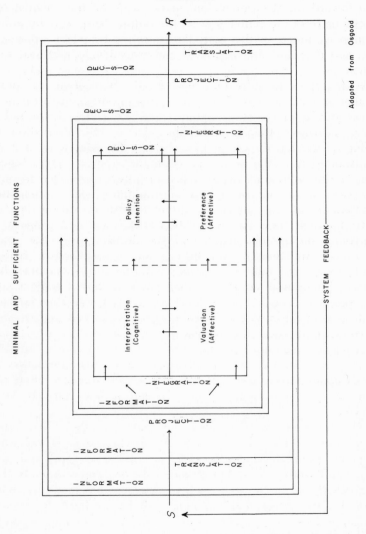

Adapted from Osgood

that has meaning for an organism; and whereby, on the other hand, the intentions of an organism are expressed and hence turned into evironmental events. By *projection* we mean the transmission of information from peripheral parts of the system toward the decision-making parts; and the transmission of decisions from the center toward the output periphery. By *integration* we mean, in this case, the processes by which information and decisions are organized and placed in operational sequence.[4]

With respect to individual behavior the translation and projection systems display certain lawful properties which do not necessarily apply to other system levels. Projection in the individual nervous system is isomorphic, that is, the information is being received at the center in essentially the same form as it is transmitted from the periphery. Moreover, the projection function in this individual nervous system is not modifiable by experience. In the long run it will be desirable to make systematic comparisons of these functions as they operate on various levels.

In a nation state the information translation and projection functions, on the one hand, and the decision projection and translation functions on the other, can be idealized as being performed by habituated and faithful civil servants. In actual operation, of course, we shall find that these functions are not performed on the state level without considerable loss or distortion of information. Projection here is not isomorphic, nor beyond modification by experience.

A certain amount of routine information is, of course, routed, to by-pass central decision-making processes. This information is acted upon more or less automatically, almost through reflex, by civil servants proceeding under general policies already laid down.

The functions of information integration and decision integration are performed in the state by specialized personnel who organize information, try to close informational gaps, and abstract and synthesize, and program for the decision-makers. In the individual and in the state (where decisions are made by individuals) the integration functions will be modified by experience, and we may expect various kinds of functioning depending on the level of general tension.

The central decision-making functions include *the cognitive interpretation of incoming information*—what is it and what are its dimensions and what are its characteristics and properties; its affective evaluation—is it good or bad, supportive or threatening, and so forth; *the formulation and explication of intention or policy;* and *the affective ordering of preference.*[5] It should be evident that the cognitive functions and affective functions, both of interpretation and of policy, are closely interactive. Their separation, in fact, can be justified only in terms of research and analytic convenience.

Basic Principles of Individual Behavior

Within a nation state the decision-making function normally resides in some form of executive institution which is composed of subordinate functional groups. Within this context it is not difficult to locate within a given state where crucial decisions of foreign policy are made. It becomes evident that key individuals usually function to determine state behavior. Thus, nation states—like all groups—are merely humans in social context, and decisions that determine state behavior are necessarily made by individuals.

In seeking to analyze state behavior, we are dealing with a difficult merging of the individual—and all his personal idiosyncrasies—with his role of state decision-maker. It would be highly desirable to design a rigorous behavior theory to encompass the whole range of systems from the individual to the state and even the world, but to date it is not entirely clear whether this task is feasible. An attempt is being undertaken separately to make more explicit—and reasonably rigorous—the translation of principles from individual to state behavior, but space precludes further consideration in this manual.[6] Here it will be sufficient to record—from Charles Osgood's Three-Stage Mediation Model of Individual Human Behavior—the basic principles upon which the attempt at translation is being made:[7]

1. Contiguity: *The shorter the time between a stimulus event and a response event the greater the increment in association.* (The sooner a child's misbehavior is followed by disapproval, or its good behavior by a word of approval, the stronger the association.)

2. Summation: *Successive increments in the association of a stimulus event with a response event summate to produce habit strength.* (The more often a child is rewarded for a given behavior, the stronger the habit is likely to become. Beyond a certain number of repetitions, however, the size of the increments will fall off.)
3. Generalization: *The habit strength generated between a stimulus event and a response event generalizes to other stimulus and other response events, the amount of such generalized habit strength being a function of* (a) *the similarity between directly associated events and* (b) *the strength of the original association.* (The child who has learned to say "thank you" at home is likely to do so elsewhere.)
4. Motivation: *Motivation combines with habit strength multiplicatively to yield performance. If either motivation or habit strength is zero, performance is likely to be zero.* (A child who has had no practice in playing the piano will not perform creditably, no matter how strong the motivation. Similarly, the child who is not motivated will fail to perform creditably, regardless of how much it has practiced.)
5. Reinforcement: *The size of the increment in association with a stimulus event and a response event varies inversely with the time interval between association and a reinforcing state of affairs, and directly with the amount of reinforcement.* (The sooner and larger the reward, the more rapidly the child will learn, up to a satiation point.)
6. Weakening: *The execution of any response produces an increment of inhibition toward making that response, such inhibition increasing with the effortfulness of the response and dissipating spontaneously with the rest.* (The longer and harder the game, the more the child will tend to taper his performance—until it has had a chance to recuperate.)
7. Selection: *Whenever two or more responses have been associated with the same stimulus, the reaction having the*

momentarily strongest habit strength will occur. (The child must decide between having its birthday cake now or saving it until friends arrive to admire it.)

8. Sensory Integration: *The greater the frequency with which stimulus events A and B have been paired in input experience, the greater will be the tendency for the central neural correlates of one, a, to activate the central neural correlates of the other, b.* (The more practice the child has at reading, the more readily it will organize letters into recognizable words without thinking about it.)

9. Motor Skill: *The greater the frequency with which response events A and B have been paired in output experience, the greater will be the tendency for the central neural correlates of one, a, to activate the central neural correlates of the other, b.* (With sufficiently frequent practice the child can play a cadenza faster than it can think about its finger movements.)

10. Representational Mediation: *Whenever a neutral stimulus is contiguous with a significate (a stimulus which, in a given situation, regularly and reliably produces a predictable response pattern), and this occurs sufficiently close to a reinforcement, the neutral stimulus will acquire an increment of association with some portion of the total behavior elicited by the significate as a representational mediation process.* (A baby will learn to associate its bottle with food and will salivate when the bottle is presented. Later in its life the child, at the sound of a siren, will look for the fire.)

This manual proceeds upon the premise that the individual, whether as a citizen or as a state leader, behaves according to these basic principles. It is in conformance with them that he perceives and responds to the various roles he plays. Some of the hypotheses derived from these principles are set forth in detail in the appendices. Appendix A contains hypotheses about the activity and behavior of states in general, and Appendix B indicates various kinds of propositions which emerged from our analysis of the 1914 crisis, culminating in World War I. We include these substantive materials in this methodological handbook in hope that they will give the student greater appreciation of the limits and potentialities of the tools of content analysis.

NOTES

[1] Cf. Kenneth E. Boulding, *Conflict and Defense: A General Theory* (New York: Harper and Brothers, 1962).

[2] Cf. Bruce M. Russett, "Cause, Surprise and No Escape," *The Journal of Politics*, 24 (1962), 3-22.

[3] From among the several uses of the word *crisis* the medical term seems to be most analogous for purposes of international conflict.

[4] Cf. Charles E. Osgood, "A Behavioristic Analysis of Perception and Language as Cognitive Phenomena," Urbana, Ill. (n.d.), pp. 3-6.

[5] Charles E. Osgood and Robert C. North, "From Individual to Nation: An Attempt to Make Explicit the Usually Implicit Process of Personifying International Relations," an unpublished manuscript (Urbana and Stanford, 1962).

[6] *Ibid.*

[7] Charles E. Osgood, "Behavior Theory and the Social Sciences," in Roland Young (ed.), *Approaches to the Study of Politics* (Evanston: Northwestern University Press, 1958), pp. 217-44; also Osgood's "Motivational Dynamics of Language Behavior" in Marshall R. Jones (ed.), *Nebraska Symposium on Motivation*, (Lincoln: University of Nebraska Press, 1957), pp. 348-424.

PART II: DATA PREPARATION

CHAPTER II*   DOCUMENTS AS A SOURCE OF DATA

Introduction

The attempt to construct and rigorously to test hypotheses in the field of political science and, more particularly, international relations, has led many investigators on an intensive search for relevant and adequate data. Some, reluctant to rely upon the traditional historical sources, have turned to the raw materials and the techniques used to test hypotheses in such fields as sociology and psychology. Depth interviews, opinion surveys, simulated gaming experiments and the like have become very much in vogue and have, of course, opened many new frontiers to scholarly probing. But the unfortunate by-product of a complete dependence upon these kinds of data is the restriction they necessarily place on the range of problems amenable to study and the kinds of hypotheses that can be tested. How, for example, would one approach the study of the effects of stress on key decision-markers? Obviously, Chairman Khrushchev and President Kennedy will not be available for depth interviews before and after, say, the Cuban crisis; and the investigator will, because of methodological constraints, deprive himself of other rather more available data emerging from the same situation.

The task confronting the behaviorially oriented scholar has been to develop an alternative strategy that would enable him to practice his craft in the ancient preserve of the historian and the traditional political scientist. Fortunately, new techniques have emerged by means of which historical documentation has become a valuable source for research requiring systematic and rigorous

---

* The major author of this chapter is Dina A. Zinnes with the colaboration of Howard E. Koch, Jr.

testing of hypotheses by quantification. As a consequence, the spectrum of problems in international relations susceptible to empirical investigation has been significantly broadened.

Inevitably, the utilization of historical documents requires that the social scientist involve himself with some of the traditional concerns of the historian. Documentation must meet certain standards if it is to serve a useful purpose, regardless of the techniques chosen to exploit it. The scholar finds it necessary, as he always has, to determine authenticity. But rigorous hypothesis testing by quantification makes further demands on data which are different and perhaps even unique. For example, when working with documentation, the historian is constantly concerned with whether "important" or "key" papers have been lost or suppressed. The addition or subtraction of a particular document could easily cast an entirely different light on the problem under study. In statistical analyses the difficulty is compounded. The investigator is obliged to determine as nearly as possible how large a segment of the total "universe" of documentation is in his hands. Beyond that, the knowledge that certain *types* of documents are missing could provide crucial information about the type of sample represented by the available documentation. From such information it could be determined, for instance, whether the sample was random or stratified, and if stratified, the basis of stratification.

The purpose of this chapter is to introduce the reader to some of the problems involved in the systematic use of documents for quantitative analysis. Much of what is discussed will be familiar territory for those trained in history. The conceptual frameworks are different, of course, and a few problems are wholly new. The present discussion is far from definitive and should be viewed as a preliminary statement, based on the experience to date of the Studies in International Conflict and Integration with the documentation of the period preceding the outbreak of the First World War. All references to specific documentation will be to that of this period. It is hoped that the discussion will stimulate others to join in the effort to find new means of exploiting historical documentation and, hopefully, to turn up solutions to some of the problems as yet unresolved.

Traditional Considerations

Of the many considerations that arise from the use of primary sources, three are of particular importance: (1) data reliability; (2) the comprehensiveness of available documentation; and (3) the qualitative characteristics of such documentation. There are numerous other, rather more specific questions which for obvious reasons cannot be treated here. For a more detailed discussion of potential pitfalls the reader is advised to turn to one of the many expositions of historical methodology produced by historians drawing on generations of experience with archival materials.

A. J. P. Taylor writes that "all sources are suspect," and adds that "little of the raw materials of history was devised especially for the use of historians; and that little is often the least reliable."[1] Few people in this world have the run of foreign office archives, and scholars are in general dependent upon what governments choose to give them. Governments, in turn, are only occasionally moved to publish their papers out of a concern for what scholars wish to know. As a result, in the realm of documentation there are many open questions, some for which there will never be answers, some of which will be answered only with the passage of time.

Of one fact we are certain: for no historical situation do we possess *all* of the documentation that existed; nor are we assured that the documentation that has been released into the public domain can as a matter of course be accepted as being entirely trustworthy. In part this may be due to bureaucratic "erosion"; in part it may be a matter of deliberate policy. The experts seem to agree that such official sinning as is done lies more in acts of omission than commission. Outright fabrication of documents is relatively rare, and such cases are usually uncovered sooner or later. On the other hand, few if any documentary series published officially (and, it follows, unofficially) can claim anything near completeness, and here the scholar has only scanty means of determining the full extent of a government's generosity.[2] These concerns, one for authenticity, the other for comprehensive coverage (or at least the knowledge of what gaps exist), are crucial for investigators intending to use documents as a basis for quantitative analysis, as they have been for tradition-ally-oriented scholars over the years.

Data Reliability:—Official documents published for scholarly consumption, while being the most *authoritative* of those in circulation, are not necessarily the most *authentic*. The French Yellow Book, issued during the First World War, is of undoubted authority, but the documents contained therein are in many cases anything but authentic. Removed by time from war-time emotional involvements and political necessities, the contents of even the privately-produced documents collections which appeared in the postwar years are superior to the special pleadings of the so-called "color books," of which the French volume is perhaps the most notorious example. For an example of what a government is capable of doing, given the right political climate, we have the magnificent *Documents Diplomatiques Francais, 1871-1914,* issued by the French Government well into the postwar years (1929 et seq.).

In approaching documents published in sets (which accounts for most of the known documentation concerned with the 1914 crisis), scholars establish in effect a hierarchy of sources, ranging from the most to the least reliable, using the latter only when the former is unavailable or contains gaps. The criteria for the ranking of documentary sources vary (and are often highly subjective), but three of the more important gross considerations are (1) the motive for publication; (2) the editor's reputation and access to archival materials; and (3) the period of publication.

The motives of the publisher to a large degree dictate just what he is willing to place in evidence, and to what extent a given collection contains either mutilations or falsifications. We have already referred to the French Yellow Book, one of a number of "color books" issued by the major (as well as some of the minor) European powers during the First World War to justify their entry into hostilities and to absolve themselves from future charges of war guilt (while underscoring evidence which might tend to locate responsibility elsewhere). Because of the outright mutilation of much of its contents, the Yellow Book is of interest mainly as an example of wartime propaganda. The British Blue

Book, while guiltless in this respect, suffers from hyper-selectivity, a fault shared by all of the color books.

After the war, far more authentic and, at the same time more comprehensive collections of documents started making their appearance under official auspices, prompted not so much by a desire to do scholars a good turn as to condemn past governments for their misdeeds and to underscore the ways in which the new regimes were "different." It was this impulse that led to the issuing of the Russian *Mezhdunarodnye otnosheniia v epokhu imperializma* and the German "Kautsky documents." The French *Documents Diplomatiques Francais*, (hereafter referred to as DDF), on the other hand, appears not to have been inspired by any particular motive, except perhaps to emulate the "publish-all" spirit of the Russians and Germans. Much of the same can be said for the preparation of the *British Documents on the Origins of the War* (BDOW), although politics may have played a part in the initiation of the project. From the above it may be inferred that no single binding generalization can be made with respect to motivation and document publication except perhaps that the circumstances under which the documents are issued are as important as the stamp "official."

If the motives of the issuing body are important in determining authenticity, so too is the editor's reputation for general competence and integrity, not to mention the degree of freedom he enjoys in selecting from the archives the materials to be included in the collection. Unfortunately, as in the case of the DDF, the names of the editors are not always supplied, and here the scholar has in their place mainly the reputation of the government concerned to guide him in assessing the merits of the documentation. Occasionally, the investigator has the explicit assurance of the editor as to the terms under which he did his work. The editors of the BDOW stated without equivocation, with respect to the possibility of suppression, that "they would feel compelled to resign if any attempt were made to insist on the omission of any document which is in their view vital or essential."[3] The best of the documents collections almost invariably contain some sort of statement laying out the "ground rules" adhered to in their preparation.

Finally, a word must be said with respect to the time of publication. At the risk of belaboring the obvious, it should be pointed out that there is considerably greater certainty of a collection's authenticity, not to say completeness, if its publication is removed in time from the events that it seeks to document. That this is so is in part due to the question of motives discussed above. But it is also due to the fact that a delay in preparation enables the compiler to examine his materials more rigorously, drawing on evidence from supplementary sources as they become available. In general, time works to the advantage of the scholar.

These then, are three of the criteria by which the authenticity of documentary series may be judged. For the investigator about to embark on a project employing quantitative analysis and using historical documents as data, the road may be easier if he establishes the integrity of the collection, as opposed to challenging the authenticity of individual documents—although this too, on occasion, may have to be done.

Comprehensiveness of available documentation:—From a given collection, how many and what kinds of documents are missing, and why? The number of documents omitted from a set is perhaps of less importance to traditional research than the question of which documents have been excluded. The requirements of quantitative analysis make both questions a significant consideration. A reasonably accurate estimate of the numerical boundaries of the available documentation is needed if the statistical operations are not to proceed from a faulty base. The dual question of which documents are missing and why are essential to an understanding of the nature of the sample.

As we have already suggested, *no* collection of documents is in any real sense complete. Consider the possibilities. For a single transaction (consisting of, say, a diplomatic report to a foreign ministry, a decision, and the resulting instruction) of the hundreds that took place during the last 30 days of peace in 1914 there may be involved: several supplementary reports (not all of which may be reproduced); a dozen or so annotations by foreign office personnel (not all of which do we have); telephone conversations (mostly unrecorded); internal and external memoranda (some of which may survive; some of which may, either through design or carelessness, be destroyed); conferences (for not all of which are there minutes); intelligence reports (many of which are still classified); preliminary drafts of the instruction (which may have been destroyed once the final draft was approved); and so on.

These losses in documentation, over which the compiler-editor has no control, may be explained simply in terms of the normal workings of a bureaucracy. There are others, however. Through any period of crisis, the day-to-day business of a foreign ministry and its diplomatic outposts continues, impeded perhaps, but never terminated. To approximate the total universe of documentation, a collection would have to contain virtually the entire contents of countless diplomatic pouches: supply orders, requests for transfer, travel orders, notifications of promotion and dismissal, instructions concerning departmental regulations or changes in codes—in short, all of the things that are a part of official housekeeping. But the editor, to keep his work within manageable proportions, must separate the wheat from the chaff. The housekeeping documents are always weeded out, as are documents of other types which the editor believes to be of no particular significance. Beyond this, the terms of reference given to an editor may call for the exclusion of certain categories of documentation. In preparing the BDOW, for example, the editors were obliged to omit any document having to do with the domestic affairs of neutral states if it was not directly related to the outbreak of war. Certain documents may be withheld from the editor altogether. Under the terms imposed by the British Official Secrets Act, some 1914 files had to await the expiration of a fifty-year period before they could be opened.

Fortunately, nearly all of the major collections contain an explanation of their scope and the criteria by which documents were selected for inclusion. The investigator may not have all that he wants, but at least he will have a fair idea of the dimensions of the materials that he has. From internal evidence, too, the scholar will occasionally find clues to the extent of a collection's coverage. If a diplomatic dispatch in a collection refers to some other communications that is not produced, obviously some confidence will be lost in the completeness of the documentation. But the investigator will save time and possibly emerge with more satisfactory results for his efforts if, whenever feasible, he selects a period for which the returns are in and the documentation has already been subjected to scholarly appraisal. Documentary detective work is best left to the archivist.

Qualitative considerations: The complex process by which a government gathers its information, makes up its mind, and communicates its decisions to its representatives abroad, gives rise to a formidable body of documentation, rich in its variety. Fortunately, owing to convention and usage, much of it falls within a relatively limited number of familiar patterns. Inasmuch as the differences between types of documents—essentially communications of one sort or another—may be of significance to a given research design, a few of the more important types should be discussed briefly. From the European crisis, we have the following main classifications:

(1) *Diplomatic Reports*: A major part of the image that a country's decision-makers have of their external environment is fashioned from the reports of envoys abroad. And it follows that a primary function of the ambassador or minister is to supply— on the basis of conversations (with foreign ministry officials and with members of the diplomatic corps), reports of attaches, surveys of the press, etc.—this vital information.

Diplomatic reports are communicated in two ways: by letter (which travels by bag) and by telegram. The latter, in 1914, was reserved in general for capsule statements of a very specific and urgent nature. A letter may contain a survey of events or an amplification of the contents of a telegram. During periods of crisis, the telegram virtually replaces the letter, and because of its length is often broken into sections and dispatched serially. Certain messages, in addition to being sent to the home government, are repeated to embassies of that country in other capitals.

The weight attached to diplomatic reports varies from country to country, depending in part upon institutional factors and occasionally the personal proclivities of key decision-makers. The "mood" in Berlin in 1914 caused the reports of some ambassadors to be favored over those of others, and the reports of the naval attaches to be particularly cherished.[4] For certain types of analysis, this could be an important consideration.

(2) *The reports of attaches* supplement those of the ambassador and, as in the case of the German naval attache in London, may even compete with the reports transmitted through ordinary channels to the foreign ministry. The reports of the military and naval attaches are customarily concerned with military matters, but in 1914 it was not uncommon to find attaches reporting and interpreting political occurrences.

(3) *Consular reports* issue from the various consular offices situated in foreign cities. In keeping with the primary duties of the consul and his staff, the reports are mainly concerned with commerce, industry, overseas trade and the like, but occasionally cover public opinion and political developments. They serve as a useful supplement to diplomatic reports inasmuch as many consulates are located away from the embassy "circuit" of the capitals, in seaports and important commercial centers, and as such are in a position to supply information on local developments and local reactions to national and international developments.

(4) *Reports of private agents* are a product of informal diplomacy, but can be of considerable importance. The agents, who are in no way formally connected with a government but who are nationals of the country in question, are selected for their influence and contacts in foreign capitals.

(5) *Communications exchanged between heads of states* are the least common form of communication between states. Such communications pass directly between sovereigns and are usually concerned with matters of the greatest urgency. Their language is personal and their appeal direct. The celebrated "Willy-Nicky" letters between the Kaiser and the Tsar at the height of the 1914 crisis are a classic example of this kind of exchange.

(6) *Memoranda* are written in the hundreds, although few find their way into document collections. In foreign office usage, they are in effect part of the organizational memory, drafted to record conversations, estimates of situations and the like, for reference purposes.

(7) *Minutes and marginal notes* consist of observations on and

recommendations concerning information contained in incoming dispatches, appended to the dispatch in question either for the record or for the benefit of those next in line to read them. In British practice, such annotations are drafted by foreign office clerks, under-secretaries, and ultimately by the foreign secretary himself; the practice in other countries follows this model. That this is so enables us to assess differences in reactions occasioned by the same message, although it should be noted that each person receiving the communication has the advantage of reading the comments of those preceding him. Marginal notes by the Kaiser Wilhelm, an inveterate and often intemperate annotater, were, in the main, instructions to subordinates or observations which tended to set the tone for subsequent judgments by others in foreign office circles. Since the comments of the Kaiser were, to say the least, spontaneous, they provide valuable insights into the states of mind of a key decision-maker under changing environmental conditions.

(8) *Instructions* are those communications by means of which foreign ministries govern the actions of their representatives. They may be sent to a single envoy, to several, or to all (in cases where an identical move is to be made at each capital); or an instruction may be sent to one embassy and repeated to others for their information only.

(9) *Circular letters* are dispatches sent to all embassies, identical in content, usually containing general information or relaying a report received by the foreign ministry from one or more of its representatives.

(10) *Formal communications to a minister of foreign affairs* by a representative of another state as a rule take three forms: the *Note*, the most authoritative of the three, which may be handed in to the minister, read to him, or both (the reply to which is not made to the ambassador, but rather to *his* foreign minister by his opposite number at home); the *note verbale*, which originates in the embassy, and is usually a simple inquiry or a record of a conversation; and the *aide memoire* which is frequently a rather detailed statement of facts concerning some matter and the arguments based thereon, in many respects simi-

lar to a Note but lacking the formalities of a signature and complimentary phrases.

These are the main categories of diplomatic documents of the 1914 period available to the investigator. There are others, originating both within and outside the narrow realm of diplomacy. Of the latter, we might mention in passing the minutes of cabinet and council meetings, parliamentary debates (which for some countries are significant, but for others are, owing to institutional factors, devoid of significance for certain types of analysis), the files of other departments, and the like, all of which have a bearing on the decision-making process in the conduct of foreign relations.

It is evident that certain kinds of documents are more appropriate for one type of research than for another. If we are concerned with the perceptions of key decision-makers, we might confine ourselves to those documents in which they tend to unburden themselves; minutes and annotations, instructions, circular letters, and the like. If our concern lies in the extent to which a prevailing climate of opinion in a segment of government affects the quality of diplomatic reporting, we might analyze, as appropriate in the case of Germany, the reports of envoys and such personal records as may exist (e.g., diaries) against the marginal notes of the Kaiser and the instructions of the foreign office. Conversely, if our interest is in the impact that diplomatic reporting has on the decision-making process, as opposed to other influences, the kinds of documents consulted might include, in addition to diplomatic reports and instructions, minutes of cabinet meetings, reports from other departments to the foreign office, parliamentary debates, etc. The kinds of documentation needed for a particular study is, in the last analysis, dictated by the requirements of the research design. A familiarity with the existing documentation will make the task of constructing a viable design that much easier.

Testing Hypotheses with Historical Documents

Because there have been few attempts to use documents as data for quantitative testing of hypotheses, many of the further problems that we will consider have not yet been adequately explored. The present discussion, growing out of experience with the documentation of the First World War, is sufficiently general for application to use of historical documents of other periods.

It has been suggested that sole reliance upon depth interviewing and other techniques of this stamp would narrow the boundaries of permissible research in international relations. It was argued, however, that it is possible to lay out a research design that would accommodate historical data as a basis for quantitative analysis. We shall discuss here one such design using documentary materials of 1914 vintage.

The following tentative hypothesis might be considered strictly for illustrative purposes:

If the incoming volume of messages for State A increases sharply over a brief time span, then the key decision-makers of A, as the recipients of this volume of messages, will perceive a sharp rise in hostility.

If the volume of incoming messages is accepted as an indicator of stress, we can define an increase in volume by a factor of two or more in 24 hours as "severe stress." The effect of severe stress on key decision-makers is expected to cause a correspondingly sharp increase in their perceptions of hostility. This formulation may not meet unanimous approval; however, as a first approximation it is adequate—at least, for the purposes of this discussion.

Before the hypothesis can be tested, the two variables must be operationalized in terms susceptible to measurement. The independent variable—message volume—might be measured by counting the number of words in all communications received by the foreign office of a given state during a specified period of time, the number of communications received by the foreign office serving as an alternate measure of message volume. The dependent variable—"perception of hostility"—will be operationalized using the techniques of content analysis, which will be discussed in the next chapter. Finally, we define the concept "key decision-maker" as any individual occupying a governmental position who can and does make decisions which are binding upon the state.

Thus our hypothesis postulates a relationship between two variables, severe stress and perception of hostility, each of which can be measured. To test the hypothesis a comparison must be made between two types of situations: one situation in which message volume doubled in 24 hours and another in which message volume remained constant. To control extraneous and irrelevant variables, both situations should be as similar as possible in all other respects. Statistically it will be desirable to have several cases of each of the two situations. Thus, at the conclusion tests could be run to determine the significance of the results.

With these restrictions in mind, the investigator now turns to an examination of the incredibly large universe of historical situations. The most obvious prerequisite for the selection of an historical period is the availability and accessibility of primary historical documentation. There are other considerations to be weighed in the final selections of an historical period and these will be discussed in subsequent sections. Let us return then to the requirements set by the hypothesis. For statistical reasons it is necessary to have either three states, or three cases of each situation. It is unnecessary that we have three *different* states; we could have the two situations obtaining three times for the same state. In fact, the use of only one state could also aid in the controlling of relevant variables. Ideally, it would be desirable, however, to find one historical period in which the two situations obtained for three states.

The selection of cases from the now smaller set of historical periods must almost be accomplished by "trial-and-error." For example, the documents for the six-week period prior to World War I are readily available. It is possible to make a rough inspection of the collection for a given state to determine whether there is a sudden increase in documents in a short span of time. This requires an actual count of the volume of messages for several spans of time, until, by trial and error, the dates for the two situations for each of the three states are found.

After the selection of the "key decision-makers," we count the frequency of occurrence for these types of statements made by them within each of the two situations and for each country. When this has been completed, statistical procedures can be employed and the significance of the results tested. The hypothesis will then be either verified or refuted.

Obviously, there are points in the above discussion where various modifications can be made, either in the hypothesis itself or in the research design. It·should, however, demonstrate that a "scientific" approach to political phenomena does not negate the use of historical documents.

Perhaps the two most serious considerations confronting the investigator who wishes to utilize historical documents for testing an hypothesis are: (1) the percentage of documents available to him of the total universe of documents for the period under study, and (2) the type of sample represented by the set of documents he intends to use. These two points are closely related. If we have the total universe of documents for a given historical period—a situation that will never arise in practice—then neither question presents any difficulty. But for any situation in which the set of documents is less than 100% both questions become relevant.

If we do not have the total universe of documentations then what portion of that universe is available? What documents are missing and why? This question is similar to one we raised earlier. For example, suppose the compiler of a set of documents published every available document for that historical period; his collection might still be incomplete if some documents had been inadvertently lost by the government through oversight, error, or misfiling. The documents in the collection were not selected on any preconceived basis, and one might say they were the result of a random process of selection. This assumes that losses or errors are random, an assumption that in some instances may not be warranted. Thus, if one individual had been particularly negligent in his duties and had lost a sizable proportion of the communications which passed through his office a certain kind of bias could be introduced. If he were the head of the war department, then the sample of documents would contain an insufficient representation of this type of communication.

The significance of the type of sample represented by a set of documents can be illustrated through a research problem. Suppose that we are interested in determining whether an international crisis affects the number of problems which a decision-maker considers. In other words, when one problem looms large, do others tend to disappear from consideration? We might then count the number of different problems which the decision-makers in each of the different states considered during the six-week period in 1914. Suppose, however, that the document collections for each country for the entire period had been compiled to include only those which were in some way related to the problem of the assassination of the Archduke. A count of the problems considered by the decision-makers would necessarily lead to the incorrect conclusion that all decision-makers were concerned only with this one problem.

Since in most instances the set of materials will not represent the entire universe of documents for the period under study, the basis of the sample is of crucial importance. The percentage of the universe represented, however, raises slightly different considerations. Actually there are two percentages involved. First there is the percentage of documents available from the total universe of documents. Secondly, there is the percentage of the type of sample. If we have a sample of all documents relating to the assassination of the Archduke, it would be desirable to know what percentage of this set is represented—is it 10%, 50%, or 85%? This is essentially a statistical question which will provide the basis for deciding on the significance of our final results.

These problems of sample and percentage of documents are compounded if the research project requires a comparison between different countries or between different historical periods. Unfortunately, the modes and criteria for the preservation of documents vary from country to country and from one historical period to another. Some foreign offices may meticulously save all communications whereas in another the destination of 25% of the communications is the wastebasket.

In addition, we must also consider the fact mentioned earlier that most document collections bear the imprint of either the government's or editor's biases.

Another problem of significance for some research is the use of different languages. This can occur within the same document collection, but most often it arises when using several collections. Suppose we wish to study the relationship of message volume to the amount and/or type of information processed by key decision-makers in times of stress. We might hypothesize that there is a curvilinear relationship. As the message volume increases, decision-makers gain more knowledge or information about the outside world, until a point is reached where the volume of incoming messages exceeds the processing capabilities of the foreign office. When this point is reached a negative relationship prevails: as message volume continues to increase decision-makers acquire less and less information from the communications. The testing of this hypothesis requires a definition and measure of message volume. If we define message volume in terms of the number of ideas or thoughts that are being received by a state in a given communication, a simple count of words would probably not be sufficient when documents are in several languages, for it may take more words in one language than in another to express the same idea. One solution to this difficulty is to take one of the documents of the set in use and have it translated into those languages used. A count of the number of words from the sample document will then provide a ratio factor which can be used to adjust the word counts from the actual documents analyzed.

Finally, we will consider a problem which is the reverse of a problem discussed earlier, namely sampling by the investigator. Undoubtedly, situations will occur in which the investigator is overwhelmed with the number of documents available for a particular historical period. What sampling criterion should be used? It is necessary to analyze carefully the problem under study to determine what types of data are necessary and relevant and which sampling technique will be appropriate. Thus an analysis of the expressions of hostility by decision-makers would, of course, restrict the use of documents to those authored by these decision-makers. On the other hand, a study of the determinants of these expressions of hostility will necessarily have to include the diplomatic reports. If we are interested in certain types of behavior of states and we assume that all states manifest essentially the same behavior under similar conditions, we might randomly choose only ten of the twenty-five countries for which we have documents. If we are, interested in a type of "stratified" sample, we could categorize states into major powers and minor powers and then randomly choose five countries from each of these categories.

The choice of randomness as the sampling criterion is usually based on the assumption that the objects to be sampled are, at least for the purposes of the study, sufficiently similar to each other, and also upon the assumption that the size of the total universe is known. Hence, by examining a certain percentage of the total universe it is possible to draw conclusions about the entire universe of objects. In practice, however, these assumptions can seldom be confirmed to the full satisfaction of the investigator.

Whether or not the documents being used are sufficiently similar to each other to warrant this assumption can be determined only within the context of a given investigation. If, for example, we are interested in the style of diplomatic language of 1914 it is probably reasonable to assume that the documents are essentially similar. A random sample from the universe of documents available could therefore be taken. However, if we are interested in the differences in diplomatic language between countries, it would only be valid to sample documents randomly within each country.

It is rarely a simple matter to decide whether documents are similar with respect to a certain variable or set of variables. It might seem reasonable to assume that a hostile expression by a decision-maker is equally probable in one document as in any other. But in fact this may not be the case. A decision-maker may feel that there are only a very few people to whom he can express his hostility. A random sample in this instance would be likely to miss these crucial documents. Some difficulties can be avoided by making a preliminary examination of the documents to determine whether the variables are randomly distributed, and by being sufficiently familiar with the background of the data being used.

Background Considerations

To avoid treacherous pitfalls, the investigator using historical documents must acquire familiarity with the historical background of the periods he has selected. An understanding of the historical background can also be of invaluable assistance in developing the research design and in properly interpreting the results.

Consider an example from 1914. The diplomatic communication structure in 1914 had a significant characteristic which pertains even today, although to a lesser extent: with only minor exceptions no two states communicated with each other directly. The communication channels might be diagrammed as in Figure II-1.

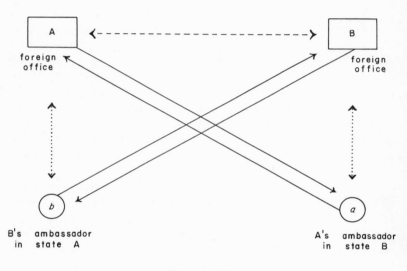

FIGURE II-1

The broken lines represent infrequent communications, while the dotted lines represent two kinds of communications: those which the ambassador is instructed to transmit to the host government, and others which were normally transmitted in other than written form. The latter often consisted of informal exchanges of information at informal conferences, luncheon discussions, cocktail-parties, and the like. While the information acquired from these meetings was usually reported back to the foreign office, the original records of these encounters may not always exist. If—without knowledge of the communication channels—we proceed to test this hypothesis that A's hostility is caused by his perceptions of B's hostility toward him by counting the hostile messages received by A directly from B, we might conclude that the proposition is false.

In fact, states in the 1914 crisis normally communicated through their respective ambassadors, and it is within this structure that the hypothesis must be tested. This requires that we count the number of hostile statements accorded to B by A's ambassador and correlate this count with A's hostility to B.

Conclusion

In this chapter we have proceeded on the assumption that within historical documents there lies a rich lode of data for the student of international relations. While documents have traditionally been a primary source for investigators, their potential value for the systematic testing of hypotheses has rarely been exhausted. But the investigator cannot approach his data uncritically: there are numerous traps into which the careless or inexperienced may fall. Some of the most important ones have been discussed already. Others, which may be unique to a given document collection, can be avoided only by a thorough knowledge of the material with which one is working.

NOTES

[1] A. J. P. Taylor, *The Struggle for Mastery in Europe, 1848-1918* (London: Oxford, 1954), p. 569.

[2] Documents are published in a number of forms. Those concerning the outbreak of the First World War appear mainly in the form of special or institutional collections (e.g., the *Special Journal* of the Russian Council of Ministers) and general collections (e.g., *British Documents on the Origins of the War*). Some documents are issued singly, usually to the press, when the occasion warrants it. And, of course, diaries, memoirs and the like constitute another important type of primary documentation. Our remarks are generally directed to documents contained in collections, by far the most important source.

[3] *British Documents on the Origins of the War*, Vol. LV, p. viii. The editors were G. P. Gooch and Harold Temperley.

[4] Gordon Craig writes that "In general, the attachés . . . were 'haloed in the Emperor's sight,'" the latter often recommending that recalled attachés be retained for special diplomatic missions. Gordon A. Craig, *The Politics of the Prussian Army, 1640-1945* (Oxford, 1956), p. 273, f. n. 1.

CHAPTER III* THE QUANTITATIVE ANALYSIS OF CONTENT

Introduction

At least two types of information helpful in studying decision-making may be obtained from documents. A journalistic or historical chronicle of events provides perspective on substantive issues involved in a decision-making situation; no rigorous technique is required for this task, as it is the salient and manifest content of messages in documents that is analyzed. Students of decision-making may also want to acquire information about characteristics of decision-makers and about interactions between them in decision-making situations in order to test hypotheses. Because this second approach demands systematically collected data, a rigorous tool, content analysis, must be used.

As a research technique, content analysis has been employed for a variety of purposes. In the study of literature this method has been used to solve questions of disputed authorship. Propaganda analysis was largely responsible for broadening the scope of content analytic studies. The method was employed by social scientists during the interwar years to explore propaganda techniques; and during World War II some United States intelligence information was derived from nonfrequency content analysis of enemy propaganda. Since World War II there have been a number of attempts to employ content analysis to study changes in symbol usage in international politics. More recently, content analysis has become a major tool of psycholinguistics, to analyze the relationship between messages and the characteristics of their users.[1]

---

* The major author of this chapter is Ole Holsti who worked from an earlier draft written by Michael Haas, and revised by Clifton Follis.

A fundamental reason for using content analysis in research on international conflict and integration has been succinctly stated by Dorwin Cartwright:

> Social and political conflicts, although often stemming from divergent economic interests and power, cannot be fully understood without studying the words employed in the interaction of conflicting groups, and the process of mediation consists largely of talking things out.[2]

Within this context, content analysis has a number of applications. It may be used to study conflicting goals or the content of ideologies. It may also be used for analysis at a somewhat different level: to gain systematic information concerning the cognitive and evaluative or affective states of those persons whose decisions are binding upon the states they represent.

In short, content analysis is used in a multitude of research investigations. There is no single "best" type of content analysis, although the trend toward asking more generic research questions in the social sciences has led to growing sophistication in design of content-analysis research.

Designing Content-Analysis Research

Content analysis research usually involves the following stages. First, the research question, theory, and hypotheses are formulated. The sample is then selected, and the categories are defined. Next, the documents are read and coded, and the relevant content is condensed onto special data sheets. After coding, items placed in each category may be scaled, whereupon counts in frequency or intensity are made. Finally, interpretations of the findings are made in light of the appropriate theory.

Formulation of the Problem

The research question is always formulated before the technique is selected. Next, narrow-gauge hypotheses and definitions of concepts are specified so that research can be reduced to specific operations.[3]

One approach to the study of international conflict is the analysis of decision-makers in crises, to ascertain the individual's images and perceptions of reality, his psychological state, and the structure and pattern of his means-end chain. For example, one proposition is that decisions to go to war are made by persons more concerned with emotional than with strategic aspects of a situation.[4] Another suggests that, as the negative affect expressed by a decision-maker increases, he will tend to seek out a form of "adjustment activity," such as increased hostility, to relieve the resulting tension. After formulating such hypotheses, the investigator may then consider relevant sampling procedures and select categories for coding his data.

Sampling

Narrowing a research problem to manageable size requires that the investigator sample the total universal of available data. A sample is taken in selecting a case and the countries to be studied and in choosing the persons and documents from which content-analysis data are to be extracted.

Both theoretical and practical considerations are involved in selection of the case and of the countries to be analyzed. The Studies in International Conflict and Integration, having formulated propositions about the behavior of decision-makers in crises, chose the 1914 European crisis because of availability and completeness of documents, and because a world war was neither consciously planned nor desired by any of the participants in advance. Although many nations were affected by the 1914 crisis, the only countries whose decision-makers' statements were content analyzed were the five major powers—Great Britain, France, Germany, Austria-Hungary, and Russia—for which relatively complete and authentic documentation was available. Italian and Serbian documents for the period were incomplete and largely unavailable at the time, except in Rome and Belgrade.

To study a state's foreign policy and decision-making, one must decide who are its decision-makers, that is, the persons empowered to bind their country by committing its resources in pursuit of goals on the international level. For sampling purposes, the "behaving state" within the international system is defined as comprising the titular head of state, the prime minister, and the foreign minister. This system has served as a basic formula which, however, has required minor variation in its application to specific research projects. For example, in the

1914 crisis and in a study of the mid-century Sino-Soviet alliance, the following decision-makers were selected as representing their respective nations.[5]

1914 DECISION-MAKERS

Germany:

Wilhelm II—Kaiser
Theobald von Bethmann-Hollweg—Imperial Chancellor
Gottlieb von Jagow—Secretary of State in the Ministry for Foreign Affairs
Alfred von Zimmermann—Under-Secretary of State in the Foreign Office

Great Britain:

George V—King of England
Mr. Herbert Asquith—Prime Minister
Sir Edward Grey—Secretary of State for Foreign Affairs
Sir Arthur Nicolson—Permanent Under-Secretary of State for Foreign Affairs

SINO-SOVIET STUDY—DECISION-MAKERS

China:

Liu Shao-ch'i—Chairman of Peoples Republic of China
Chou En-lai—Chairman of the People's Council
Chen Yi—Foreign Minister
Mao Tse-tung—Chairman of the Communist Party
Kuo Mo-jo—Communist Party spokesman

Soviet Union:

Leonid Brezhnev—President of the Soviet Union
Nikita Khrushchev—Premier
Andrei Gromyko—Foreign Minister

The sampling of types of sources depends upon the research problem. A primary source is a document which the decision-maker has written; a secondary source is one in which the decision-maker is quoted or paraphrased by an authority who is considered reliable. Experience suggests that the following rules for selecting sources may prove useful:

1. Permissible primary sources:
   a. Any official communication from one government to another.
   b. Diplomatic instructions, intelligence and military reports, departmental memoranda, records or cabinet and council meetings, parliamentary debates, memoirs and diaries, *if* issued by bona fide decision-makers.
   c. A statement found in a document drafted by or under the direction of one of the decision-makers.

2. Permissible secondary sources:
   a. Ambassador reports or newspaper accounts based on conversations with key decision-makers, *if* the ambassador or writer quotes or paraphrases the decision-maker and does not record his own inferences.

Some document collections, notably the so-called "color books" of the 1914 crisis, have been tampered with and therefore are not suitable sources. In addition, documents *written at the time*—not recollections—are used; diaries are therefore to be preferred to memoirs, which in many cases have later been edited. Such decisions are made *before* the coder begins his work.

At this stage, the investigator has narrowed down—according to his theoretical interests and the rules of data quality—the messages which he must submit to content analysis. The next step is to determine a classificatory system for his data by constructing categories into which the data are to be placed.

Category Construction

The purpose of defining a category is to permit a classification of data on the basis of selected concepts. It then becomes possible to measure the intensity and frequency of occurrence of variables represented by each category.

Any category must be evaluated in terms of such standard criteria as validity, reliability, and objectivity.[6] *Validity* represents the extent to which an instrument measures what it is intended to measure. A category is valid when two independent measures of the same phenomenon yield similar results. To achieve *reliability*, the categories must be so constructed that when the same research process is repeated, it will reproduce results within stated confidence limits. There are two types of reliability. "Intercoder reliability" refers to the degree of agreement between different coders at the same time, whereas "intracoder reliability" measures the test-retest stability of an individual coder over time. Finally, a category is *objective* when it yields unbiased data independent of the idiosyncracies of data collectors. Hence, validity, reliability, and objectivity are a function of category construction, which, in turn, determines the effectiveness of the coding and scaling operations.

The perceptions which are catalogued for analysis can be divided into two broadly defined groups—affective or evaluative and cognitive or perhaps more properly, denotative.[7] An affective or evaluative perception suggests the attitudinal component in an expression. On the other hand, a cognitive perception mainly serves to describe a condition or an action. Denotative perceptions might include policy condition, resolution of conflict, and capability; affective perceptions might include power, friendship, hostility, satisfaction, and frustration. Other categories might also be pertinent to a given study. For illustrative purposes, each of the categories listed above is defined with examples drawn from the studies of the 1914 crisis and of the Sino-Soviet alliance.

A *perception of policy condition* suggests actions, past or present, and behavior which fall on a means-ends chain.[8] It includes elements such as goals, aims, preferences, choices, and the means by which a state reaches, or proposes to reach, these goals. A state's goals may refer either to long-range and ultimate objectives or to concrete, immediate goals and means for pursuing and attaining these objectives.

Examples:

Prime Minister Herbert Asquith told Parliament (July 29, 1914): "As the House is aware, a formal Declaration of War was issued yesterday by Austria against Serbia."

Premier Khrushchev commented on America's stated policy concerning U-2 flights (May 20, 1960): ". . . the President of the United

States promises . . . merely a temporary 'suspension' of flights till January 1961."

The *perception of resolution of conflict* involves two aspects: (1) the assessment of the possible mode of resolution, and (2) expectations as to the consequences following from a resolution of conflict. It suggests the concern expressed by a participant as to the nature and consequence of conflict resolution.

Examples:

Sir Arthur Nicolson judged the probable means of resolving the impending conflict (July 28, 1914): ". . . in that case (of Austria-Hungary invading Serbia) all hope of a peaceful solution will vanish."

Kaiser Wilhelm II, on the eve of the outbreak of World War I (July 30, 1914) predicted that: ". . . if we are to bleed to death, England shall at least lose India."

A *perception of capability* includes passive, non-volitional assertions in such matters as the quantitative possession of economic wealth, military weapons, number of troops. This category involves numerical, but not qualitative, estimates of state capability. It applies when the item is a resource which may be committed in pursuing a policy condition.

Examples:

French Minister of Foreign Affairs assessed Belgian capabilities (July 28, 1914): ". . . the recall of the classes of 1912, 1911, and 1910 . . . with the class of 1913, would bring the man-power of the Belgian army to 100,000 men."

Premier Khrushchev told the Supreme Soviet (January 15, 1960): "A rocket launched by the Soviet Union in the direction of the moon became the solar system's first artificial planet."

The category *perception of power* includes statements which assess the relative strength and weakness of participants within the international system. This assessment is qualitative, and not quantitative or numerical.

Examples:

In a note (June 27, 1914) to the German government, the government of Austria-Hungary evaluated Turkish power: "Turkey . . . constituted a powerful counterweight to Russia and the Balkan States."

Li Fu-ch'un stated (January 1, 1960) that: "There is no doubt but that we will be able to leap forward continuously."

A *perception of friendship* is the sense of approbation and positive disposition expressed between participants. It suggests affective ties between states in supporting the fulfillment of objectives.
Examples:

Emporer Franz Joseph wrote the Kaiser Wilhelm II (July 2, 1914): "I should have been glad to express to you personally my heartfelt gratitude. . . ."

An editorial in the *Peking Review* (April 7, 1961) stated, referring to Premier Sukarno, that: "Ever fresh in the minds of our people are his passionate words on the friendly relations between China and Indonesia which he spoke during his visit to China."

A *perception of hostility* is defined as the sense of enmity and negative affect which one participant expresses for another. [9] It indicates the basic attitude of obstructionism *vis a vis* the objectives of another participant.
Examples:

Kaiser Wilhelm described British policy (July 30, 1914): ". . . she (England) twists the noose of our political and economic destruction."

An editorial in *Jen-min jih-pao* declared (January 15, 1960): "People's Republic of China resolutely opposes the Japan-U.S. military alliance."

The category *perception of satisfaction* indicates the feeling of success and contentment, the sense of being pleased and fulfilled as the recipient of an action. It focuses upon one's own positive feelings about his situation within the system.
Examples:

Austria, in a message to Germany, noted a gratifying change in Bulgarian policy (June 27, 1914): "But of greatest importance is the fact that Bulgaria has awakened from the spell cast by Russia."

Premier Khrushchev stated (May 19, 1960): "I am happy to say that a common desire was revealed to continue to exert efforts for the development of our relations in every way."

The category *perception of frustration* involves the sense of failure and disappointment expressed by a participant, resulting from constraint in the fulfillment of his policies. It suggests anxiety and discomfort, and stresses the participant's negative feelings about himself and his own situation within the system. Examples:

Austria declared (June 27, 1914): ". . . the situation as it exists today . . . when looked at from the point of view of the Triple Alliance, can not be described as at all favorable."

Kuo Mo-jo announced (May 21, 1960): "We absolutely cannot tolerate U.S. imperialism."

Coding[10]

The Studies in International Conflict and Integration have chosen themes, rather than words, as the basic recording unit of analysis. The coders develop skill in reducing paragraphs and sentences into "atomic themes" or unit-perceptions, that is, assertions which themselves cannot be broken down further. The following examples are themes drawn from documents:

1. "I understand that Russian Minister for Foreign Affairs has proposed friendly exchange of views to Austrian Government. . . ."
2. "The Greater Serbian propaganda finally resulted in the crime of Sarajevo."

The unit-perception is conceived in terms of three separate actor-levels with respect to the action or affect described in the given perception. The basic unit statement which is to be coded —and later scaled—is composed of (1) the *perceiver* of the action or affect expressed; (2) the actor whose affect or action is being *perceived;* (3) the *target* or recipient of the action or expressed affect; and (4) the *descriptive-connective,* or the nature of the action or affect expressed between actors.

The relationship between these components is stated symbolically in Figure III-1. The arrow represents the direction of

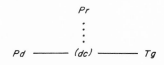

FIGURE III-1

the action and/or affect which is expressed, while the series of vertically aligned dots indicates the line of perception and stimulus. The descriptive-connective *(dc)* serves as the scalable portion of the unit-statement or assertion; it also suggests the nature of the variable.

The cardinal rule in coding and preparing unit-statements for scaling is that no assertion must have more than *one* perceiver, *one* perceived, *one* target, and *one* descriptive-connective. However, in a given unit-statement, for example, "The war is being fought vigorously," neither a perceived nor a target may be immediately apparent. This type of situation is handled by labelling both the perceived and the target as either "general" or "unspecified," whichever is the more appropriate. Despite this qualification, *all* unit-statements will contain a definite perceiver of the action and/or affect as well as a descriptive-connective, since a given actor must necessarily be the source of the perception and the assertion must have a determinable content.

In addition to a change in any one of the actor-levels, the occurrence of a new category-dimension will be indicative of the boundary of the particular unit-perception. For example, a text reading, "The intention of Austria, as well as that of Germany, is the ultimate annihilation of Serbia," should be coded as two separate policy conditions:

1. "The intention of Austria . . . is the ultimate annihilation of Serbia."
2. "The intention of Germany . . . is the ultimate annihilation of Serbia."

The last example is illustrative of a basic principle: if a new perceiver, a new perceived, or a new target of perception occurs, then a new unit-perception begins.

The following "cutoff rules" will suggest how to distinguish the end of one theme and the beginning of another:

1 A theme under no circumstances extends beyond the end of a paragraph.

2. A new perception (or theme) occurs when either:
   a. the "perceiver" changes,
   b. the "perceived" changes,
   c. the "target of the perception" changes, or,
   d. the category changes.

Content analyzed data may be recorded and stored on many types of coding sheets. The coding sheets used by the Studies in International Conflict and Integration summarize information abstracted from the document and identify relevant actors. The coders reproduce the text—to avoid loss of context—from which themes are extracted. Each theme, which must be reproduced verbatim, is entered as a "capsule statement" with elisions, insertions, and quotation marks clearly indicated. An example of a coding sheet is exhibited in Figure III-2.

The coder first reads through the complete document, then rereads each paragraph; in languages where there are no paragraphs, about two column-inches are equivalent to one paragraph. When a coder locates a perception in the document, he fills out a coding sheet in the following manner.

1. The first line below the title, DENOTATIVE PERCEPTIONS, calls for the "Author of statement"; this is the same as the person who is author of the message. The "Recipient of statement" is the person or country to whom the message has been sent. "Person quoted" refers to the individual quoted or paraphrased by the document author. If the person quoted orally communicated his message to someone, the "someone" is the "Interlocutor."

2. Line three calls for the "Source" where the document is printed and the date when it originated and/or was printed.

3. Lines four and five call for information about who is talking about whom. If Khrushchev states that Russian policy is peaceful coexistence, the "Perceiver" and "Perceived" is the author—Russia, in the person of its decision-maker, Khrushchev—because Russia is perceiving her own policy. However, if Khrushchev tells the General Assembly that he believes that the United Nations was deliberately slow in punishing aggressors, then the "perceiver" is Russia (author) whereas the "perceived" is the recipient (United Nations)—Russia would be perceiving someone else's policy.

4. The next line calls for the "Target of perception," that is, the object toward which the policy or action is directed. In the above example, the United Nations is directing its policy at the Congo (the target).

FIGURE III-2

DENOTATIVE PERCEPTIONS: A__ B__ C__

Author of document <u>Khrushchev</u> Person quoted <u>N/A</u> Receipent of document <u>Press Conference</u> Interlocutor <u>N/A</u> Source <u>Pravda</u> <u>60-5-19</u> "Perceiver": Auth. <u>x</u> Recip.___ Pers. quoted___ Interloc.___ Other___ "Perceived": Auth. <u>x</u> Recip.___ Pers. quoted___ Interloc.___ Other___ "Target" of perception <u>U.S.A.</u> This perception is stimulated by an event in the PAST<u>xx</u> PRESENT____ FUTURE____

Text: Of course, it is for President Eisenhower to decide whether to send or not to send his planes. It is another question whether they will be able to fly over our territory. This is decided by us, and very definitely for that matter. We shall shoot these planes down; we shall administer shattering blows at the bases whence they come and at those who have set up these bases and actually dispose of them.

Capsule statement(s):
A 1. This [whether or not US will be able to fly over the USSR] is DECIDED by us.
   2. We (USSR) SHALL SHOOT these planes (US) down . . .
   3. . . . we (USSR) SHALL ADMINISTER shattering blows at the bases whence they (US planes) come . . .
   4. . . . we (USSR) SHALL ADMINISTER shattering blows . . . at those who have set up these bases and actually dispose of them (bases).
B
C

A: PERCEPTION OF POLICY CONDITION
C: PERCEPTION OF CAPABILITIES
B: PERCEPTION OF
   RESOLUTION OF CONFLICT

5. In the space marked "text" the coder types out in full the paragraph from which the theme is extracted. The purpose of

recording the text is to establish the context for future reference.

6. In the space reserved for "Capsule statement," the coder records the atomic theme. The following form is preferred—a direct quotation with deletion marks for the elements which do not belong to that theme.

Reliability

The reliability of coded data is partially a function of the training during which coders familiarize themselves with the concepts used. Validity of the data, as well as ability to generalize the results, is directly related to the level of reliability. Thus, checks on reliability are necessary at various intervals during a study to assess both intracoder and intercoder agreement. During training, coders are given reliability tests consisting of sample passages to be coded. Reliability checks on an actual study are made at the beginning and end of research. Tests consist of a multicoding of materials which have actually been coded during the study.

Reliability may be computed by one of several formulas, each designed for a specific situation. The simplest to compute is the formula for the two-coder situation.

$$R = \frac{2(C_{1,2})}{C_1 + C_2}$$

The number of category assignments on which all coders agree is divided by the sum of all category assignments by all coders.[11]

What is to be done when intercoder agreement figures are below an acceptable level? Research directors may continue to train coders, redefine and tighten categories, or adjust the number of categories for which a single coder is responsible. Often intercoder agreement is low because coders do not agree on the meaning of categories; this occurs when the category definition with which coders are working is either too vague or prolix. If a category consists of many components, or sub-categories, it is best to make each component explicit. A category that has many components, or one that has several components found with high frequency in coding, should be split into two or more separate categories. Reliability is higher the fewer decisions a coder has to make.

Too much emphasis on reliability may make coders unduly conservative. They may code only what they are sure others would include, omitting borderline cases from the sample. If the loss from conservatism is too great, multiple coding of the same documents is the only way to keep both reliability and richness of data; however, the cost of research is materially increased. Researchers may find that multiple coding of a representative sample is advantageous; "low reliability" and "high reliability" data may then be compared to determine the extent of bias due to conservatism.

Summary and Conclusion

Content analysis is a term used to describe a wide variety of research techniques, all of which are used for systematically collecting, analyzing, and making inferences from messages. Thus the decisions, (1) whether to use content analysis, and (2) which of the many techniques to adopt, are made on the basis of the investigator's problem.

The payoff in research consists of inferences drawn from the evidence to test hypotheses. The meticulousness in designing and conducting research increases the confidence in conclusions drawn on the basis of inference.

From the various kinds of evidence derived through content analysis—including qualitative evidence, frequencies, trends, contingencies, and intensities—several types of inferences may be drawn. Currently much content analysis research is devoted to inferring from a text the characteristics of its authors. Intentions, foci of attention, and psychological states of decision-makers would be relevant in this application. Inferences can be made concerning matters of which the writer may not be cognitively aware; for example, the frustration or satisfaction level of a decision-maker may be determined. In addition, one may detect changes in behavior from the individual's usual pattern.

The investigator may, from the same kinds of evidence, also draw inferences other than those concerning the characteristics of authors. A nonfrequency technique has been used to reconstruct the end-means chains of decision-makers from policy condition themes.[12] In the construction of end-means chains, inconsistency within a single decision-maker's behavior pattern and points of conflict between decision-makers are spotlighted.

The investigator interested in drawing inferences from changes in the hostility level of a state or group of states may plot trends, using either the frequency or intensity of statements, or both, as his index. From rising or falling levels of hostility, analysts may then be able to make inferences about the likelihood of conflict. On the other hand, the investigator would use contingency analysis to determine the relation between indices of two variables, such as satisfaction and frustration. From the relationship between these variables he may then draw further inferences concerning tension levels.

NOTES

[1] The various uses of content analysis are discussed in Bernard Berelson, *Content Analysis in Communications Research* (Glencoe: The Free Press, 1952). Examples of content analysis research may be found in Harold D. Lasswell, *Propaganda Techniques in the World War* (New York: A. A. Knopf, 1927); Harold D. Lasswell and Dorothy Blumenstock, *World Revolutionary Propaganda* (New York: A. A. Knopf, 1939); Alexander L. George, *Propaganda Analysis* (Evanston: Row, Peterson, 1959); Harold D. Lasswell, Daniel Lerner, and Ithiel de Sola Pool, *The Comparative Study of Symbols* (Stanford: Stanford University Press, 1952); Ithiel de Sola Pool, (ed.) *Trends in Content Analysis* (Urbana: University of Illinois Press, 1959); and Charles E. Osgood, *The Measurement of Meaning* (Urbana: University of Illinois Press, 1957).

[2] Dorwin P. Cartwright, "Analysis of Qualitative Material," in Leon Festinger and Daniel Katz, (eds.) *Research Methods in the Behavioral Sciences* (New York: The Dryden Press, 1953), p. 422.

[3] The various types of propositions about the relationship between variables is discussed in Part II, Chapter 3 of David Easton, *The Political System* (New York: A. A. Knopf, 1953).

[4] Dina Zinnes, Robert C. North, and Howard E. Koch, Jr., "Capability, Threat and the Outbreak of War," in James N. Rosenau (ed.) *International Politics and Foreign Policy* (New York: The Free

Press of Glencoe, 1961), pp. 469-82. Hypotheses of the Studies in International Conflict and Integration have been catalogued in Howard E. Koch, Jr., Robert C. North, and Dina Zinnes, "Some Theoretical Notes on Geography and International Conflict," *The Journal of Conflict Resolution*, 4 (1960), 4-14; Jane Connell, Howard E. Koch, Jr., Robert C. North, and Stephen Tallent, "A Statement of Progress," multigraphed: Stanford University, October 1, 1959; and Robert C. North, Howard E. Koch, Jr., and Dina Zinnes, "The Integrative Functions of Conflict," *The Journal of Conflict Resolution*, 4 (1960), 355-74.

5 In the 1914 study, similar lists of decision-makers—not included in the example above—were drawn up for France, Russia, and Austria-Hungary. Owing to the structure of the Government of the People's Republic of China, it was necessary to include—in addition to the head of state, head of government, and foreign minister—certain other decision-makers and sources, which were clearly authorized to make policy statements, or, which reflected official policy. These additional sources included the statements of Mao Tse-tung, Chairman of the Communist party, Kuo Mo-jo, the Party spokesman, and certain anonymous editorials from official newspapers and journals.

6 Fuller discussions of validity and reliability may be found in Helen Peak, "Problems of Objective Observation," in Festinger and Katz, *op. cit.*, pp. 283-96.

7 For a somewhat different use of the terms "cognitive," "affective," and "evaluative," see Talcott Parsons, *The Social System* (Glencoe: The Free Press, 1951). These terms are still debated among social scientists; their usage in this handbook is operational rather than definitive, and thus subject to further refinement.

8 Certain qualities of policy conditions may be isolated, measured, and analyzed, including: *Change of Status Quo*, the degree to which a policy is calculated to alter existing relations between states; *specificity*, the focused, specific and immediate aspect of a policy; *general affect*, the general emotive content in the expression of a policy condition; and *violence*, the extent to which a policy implies violence as a means.

9 Three facets of the concept of hostility may be distinguished: (1) the *affective* element defined and illustrated above; (2) the *action* element found in the assertion, "Germany has invaded Belgium"; and (3) the *threat* element present in the statement, "We will bury you." The definitions offered in this handbook are of a general nature, and finer distinctions must sometimes be made for operational purposes.

10 A comprehensive discussion of coding may be found in Michael Haas, "Thematic Content Analysis in the Study of Diplomatic Doc-

uments," Studies in International Conflict and Integration, mimeo.: Stanford University, Revised version, Nov. 30, 1961.

[11] A further discussion may be found in W. S. Robinson, "The Statistical Measurement of Agreement," *American Sociological Review,* 22 (1957), 17-25.

[12] Robert C. North, "Fact and Value in the 1914 Crisis," paper presented to the Conference on Decision-making in Crises, Palo Alto, California, January 12, 1962.

CHAPTER IV

MEASURING THE INTENSITY OF ATTITUDES AND BEHAVIOR

1.

Introduction

One technique which is useful for differentiating perceptions of actors within an international system is the Q-Sort method of scaling.[1] The Q-Sort method has been used primarily as a means of objectifying subject evaluation in "personality assessment and psychiatric research."[2] It was originally suggested to the Stanford Studies in International Conflict and Integration as an effective and quick way of measuring the *intensity* of variables which describe crises.

The adoption of this technique grew out of exploratory work in measuring the intensity of hostility expressed by participants in the 1914 crisis. Soon it became apparent that both the affective and the action elements common to international political behavior could be measured. It was felt that so-called "tension profiles" over time, based upon a series of measurable variables, might be constructed for comparative and analytic purposes. In addition, indices of affective and behavioral expression would permit a comparison of patterns of variation in different types of conflict situations. Finally, hypotheses and theories relating to international crisis were developed, which could be retested and refined in a series of historical case studies involving conflict.

The Q-Sort technique has proven useful in measuring and comparing intensities of expression across a series of variables, thus serving as an effective tool in moving from the simple frequency to the intensity level of analysis. This quantification of intensity levels will make it possible to apply mathematical

---

* The major author of this chapter is M. George Zaninovich.

models and algebraic formulas in order to describe the behavior of states in international crises.

Dimensionality of Variables

The initial task in research of this kind is to decide upon the nature of variables or qualities of crisis which are to be measured.[3] The selection of variables is determined in large part by the theoretical framework and the tentative set of hypotheses of the particular study.

In using the Q-Sort, the major pre-requisite for scalability is a conceptualization and treatment of a variable in terms of a *least-to-most intense* expression of its defined content. The midpoint or mode of such a dimension or continuum should not be thought of as "neutral," that is, as being of zero value. On the contrary, the mode is defined as an average expression of intensity within the universe of statements presently before the scaling judge. For applying the Q-Sort, no set of detailed scaling rules or criteria are required for any of its nine categories of differentiation. The scaling judge need only be capable of distinguishing the relative more-or-less of the particular variable as it has been defined. However, the lack of any such exact criteria requires the scaling judge to internalize the definition of a variable sufficiently to enable him to make not only numerous, but also consistent decisions within the universe which is being scaled.

The dimensionality of a variable, that is, establishing its plus and minus polar extremes, is not achieved in the Q-Sort by the definition of the variable. On the contrary, this dimensionality is established by the statistical device of the Q-Sort which suggests a least-to-most intense expression of any variable. Therefore, a single concept (such as hostility) may be defined only in terms of its modal, average, or characteristic expression and not in terms of its extreme variations. Hence, the dimensionality of a scalable variable is not a function of the definition of that variable but of the measuring instrument which is employed.

Some scaling techniques define and prescribe the dimension of a variable in primarily substantive terms. For example, the dimension hostility-friendship may be considered a scalable variable with its dimensionality being acquired by defining *two distinct concepts,* hostility and friendship. In this instance, the given pair of concepts would be treated as being empirically, mutually exclusive, which makes it impossible to determine an empirical relationship between hostility *and* friendship.[4] However, if the Q-Sort method were applied, the variable hostility would acquire a dimensionality of its own by the Q-Sort device of a least-to-most intense expression. Assuming that friendship is treated in a similar manner, a positive correlation might be discovered in a given case between hostility and friendship, a finding which might be of the utmost importance in a particular analysis. In this way, the investigator does not lose information about the empirical relationship between any two variables.

The variable, in brief, must not be so narrowly prescribed that it does not permit effective treatment on such a continuum, that is, as a dimension defined in terms of a least-to-most intense expression of its content. On the other hand, the definition should be sufficiently precise to allow respectable reliability and agreement among scaling judges.

Basic Measurable Units

To achieve precision and reliability in scaling, the basic measurable or recording unit must be rigorously defined. The basic unit must be so constructed as to enable the investigator to isolate that element in an assertion which has affected a set of scaling judgments. This objective requires that compound statements be reduced to primitive assertions, which introduces the problem of the homogeneity of statements placed before the scaling judge.

The basic unit-statement or assertion which is to be scaled must be delimited by these components: (1) the *perceiver,* (2) the *perceived,* (3) the *target,* and (4) the *descriptive-connective,* which determines the nature of the variable.[5] As indicated in the chapter on content analysis, any given unit-statement or theme must have no more than one of each of these components. In this way, the various actors involved may be clearly designated and a single variable may be isolated.

For clarity and precision in scaling, it is *essential* that only *one descriptive-connective* be included in any one unit-statement. Otherwise, the investigator would never be certain which of several descriptive-connectives affects the scaling judgment. This guarantees that only one variable is present in the given assertion.[6] For example: if a judge were to scale the rather complex statement, "The treacherous Chinese have sent military forces into Korea in order to exterminate the Korean people," for the variable hostility, the investigator would not know if the scaling judgment were primarily affected by "treacherous Chinese," "have sent military forces," or "exterminate the Koreans." This problem is most effectively handled during the time that unit-statements or themes are coded and prepared for the scaling operation. The above compound statement should be broken down into three separate assertions or unit-statements, thus: "The Chinese are treacherous," "The Chinese have sent military forces into Korea," and "The Chinese want to exterminate the Koreans."[7] Handling compound statements in this manner helps to achieve a consistency within the universe of statements being scaled, which, in turn, increases the possibility of respectable reliability in the scaling process.

The separation of a compound statement into its primitive units of assertion reflects two distinguishable categories of descriptive-connectives. The one may be designated as *affective* or evaluative, and the other as the element of *activity* or behavior. Accordingly, two generic elements would be scalable in any population of unit-statements—*affect* and *action*. Operationally, these two categories should roughly parallel adjectives and/or predicate adjectives and verb constructions respectively.[8] Each of these generic categories requires different types of variables for scaling purposes, for example, hostility and satisfaction for affect, and specificity and violence for action. *Both* the unit-statements and the variables must be prepared and selected in such a way as to avoid the confusion of these two essentially distinct categories.

The preparation of the sample of unit-statements also requires that all references to particular countries, decision-makers, and geographic locales be eliminated. This "masking" of content serves to reduce any prejudicial elements which a particular judge might introduce into his scaling operation. The masking of statements involves the simple procedure of substituting a letter for a given country—the symbol "X" for the designation "Austria." For example, the assertion "The Soviet Union has mobilized against Germany" would be converted to "X has mobilized against Y." The masked assertion which is to be scaled is typed upon a blank sheet of paper with a conveniently located identifying number. This identifying number should correspond to its counterpart on the coding sheet upon which other information pertaining to the statement is recorded.

Distribution of the Q-Sort Scale

The Q-Sort method of scaling is based upon a *rank-order* of the given universe of statements being scaled. This rank-order, for the sake of convenience and economy, is reduced or "forced" into a nine category differentiation. Hence, what is derived is not a rank-order of assertions or unit-statements as such, but rather a *rank-order of classes* of statements in relation to the particular universe of assertions which is set before the scaling judge. These nine categories also function as values which become attributes of unit-statements within the universe being scaled. Hence, each point along the scale is logically designated a *category-value,* which indicates its double function.

The distribution of unit-statements over the nine categories is prescribed or forced to help insure that scaling judges will make the necessary fine distinctions. The prescribed distribution used by the Q-Sort method of scaling is set forth in Table IV-1.

TABLE IV-1

Category (y)	1	2	3	4	5	6	7	8	9	(value)
Percentage (x)	5	8	12	16	18	16	12	8	5	(number)

The predominant quality which this Q-Sort distribution possesses is that of *symmetry* or balance, with its mode represented by the "bulge" in the middle categories. Accordingly, the scaling judge will be required to place an equivalent number of statements in categories 1 and 9, 2 and 8, and so on.

The distribution of the Q-Sort is based upon the assumption that, in a representative sample of a given phenomenon, a greater number of units will manifest an "average" or moderate expression of a quality than an extreme expression. This assumption indicates that the Q-Sort distribution tends to approximate what is known in statistics as a "normal curve."[9] However, it also reveals some significantly different qualities from those which a statistically normal distribution possesses.[10] The forced distribution of the Q-Sort is not "realistic" or "true" in any sense, that is, indicating some irrefutable underlying reality. It is simply a statistical device for scaling which compels judges to work hard at making discriminations.

The forced symmetrical distribution of the Q-Sort allows the comparison of intensity across variables as well as over time. Since the modal expression of any one of a set of measurable variables would be represented by the category-value of 5, it becomes possible to compare their intensities of expression on the basis of deviation from this mode. For example: If hostility and friendship are both scaled for intensity, and we find that for a given time-unit the value of friendship is 5.50 and that of hostility is 4.30, then we can say that the intensity of friendship in this situation was high and that of hostility was low; we may also conclude that friendship was more intensely expressed than was hostility. This comparability is achieved by the reduction of hostility and friendship to a *common measure* of varying intensity by forcing symmetrical distribution in the scaling process.

In addition, the forcing of distribution minimizes the possibility of developing unduly rigid and "absolute critera"[11] in making scaling judgments. It also serves to avoid the distortion which the idiosyncratic categorizing proclivities of a scaling judge might introduce.[12] If a scaling judge transfers a set of absolute criteria from one universe of unit-statements to another, this transfer tends to bias the relative rank-ordering of the second universe. In the Q-Sort, the absolute standard is set by a statistical device, that is, by the prescribed distribution, and not by establishing rigorous criteria for exclusion or inclusion of unit-statements within any given category.

The size of the universe of unit-statements or assertions for scaling will vary with the purpose of a given study. Experience has indicated that as few as 25 and as many as 1,500 unit-statements can be scaled successfully. The powers of concentration of the particular set of scaling judges, as well as the clarity of the masked assertions, should be considered in deciding upon the size of the universe to be scaled. To determine how many unit-statements are to be placed within scale-categories, the number of statements within the given universe should be multiplied by the percentage allocation for each category.

The scaling judge should always keep in mind that the Q-Sort method implements a relative and not an absolute scale of differentiation. The judgment must be made in terms of the relation of one statement to another, or to the universe of assertions which is currently before the scaling judge, and *not* in terms of rigid criteria brought in from outside the set of phenomena. The Q-Sort method of scaling assumes that each universe of unit-statements manifests its own unique expression of a given variable; this is determined by the scaling process and can only be established by agreement among a set of scaling judges. The forced symmetrical distribution of the Q-Sort serves both to impose a necessary discipline upon the set of judges and to provide a common base for comparing the intensity of a set of variables.

Scaling Procedure and Reliability

Before the actual scaling process begins, a clear definition of the variable must be provided. The set of scaling judges should prepare themselves by thoroughly discussing the definition of the variable. In addition, a few statements from a related but not the same population of unit-statements should be used for "trial run" scaling operations. This assures that the variable is viewed in the same manner by the set of scaling judges, and also provides some advance indicators of reliability and agreement among the scaling judges to be used. Preliminary reliability coefficients should be derived during this training phase; in addition, those assertions upon which there is significant disagreement should be inspected and discussed by the judges. Once the actual scaling operation is underway, the scaling judges *must not consult* with one another with respect to the universe of unit-statements which is currently being scaled.[13]

The scaling operation itself may be divided for convenience into two distinct phases. *Phase 1:* The scaling judge should "freely" place all unit-statements or assertions in any one of the nine available scale-categories, keeping in mind the general nature of the distribution.[14] *Phase 2:* Once this operation is completed, resulting in a rough approximation of the prescribed distribution, the assertions should be *re*read in order that the scaling judge may verify his initial impressions. During this *re*-reading, the scaling judge should make the necessary adjustments to accommodate the universe of unit-statements to the prescribed distribution of the Q-Sort. In some instances, even a third and fourth reading of the statements may be necessary. Experience suggests that only in rare instances is it necessary to move a unit-statement more than one category up or down the scale. Imposing such a constraint avoids an excessive reshuffling of the unit-statements; it also presumes the accuracy of the initial reaction by a scaling judge to a given assertion.

When the proper distribution has been achieved, each unit-statement or assertion assumes the value of the category in which it is placed. These category-values for unit-statements must then be recorded within properly identified cells on appropriate scaling data forms.

The reliability of the data is established by the degree of agreement among a set of scaling judges for the universe of statements being considered. The level of reliability is a function of three factors operative in the scaling process: (1) the power of concentration and span of attention which the scaling judges possess, (2) the clarity and simplicity of the masked unit-statements, and (3) the effectiveness and duration of the training of the scaling judges. The degree of agreement is determined among judges by computing both an *inter-judge correlation* and a *composite reliability*.

The inter-judge correlation may be computed by applying this formula: $r = \dfrac{\Sigma d^2_{ip}}{K}$, in which i and p represent the two scaling judges.[15] The constant, K, is a function both of the prescribed distribution and of the total number of unit-statements which is scaled. On the basis of the Q-Sort distribution presented in Table 1 above, a formula for determining the value of the constant may be stated as follows: $K = x_1 (y_1 - y_9)^2 + x_2 (y_2 - y_8)^2 + x_3 (y_3 - y_7)^2 + x_4 (y_4 - y_6)^2$, in which the x values refer to the number of statements prescribed for the designated category, and the y values represent the number defining the rank of the category.[16] For example, the numerical value of K is 864 for 100 unit-statements, while it is 4320 for a universe of 500 statements. The value of K would thus be increased or decreased in proportion to the number of unit-statements or assertions in the given universe.

The range of possible inter-judge correlation scores constitutes a spectrum from —1.00 to +1.00, with any value above 0.00 being somewhat better agreement than that achieved by purely random scaling. In other words, if an average of inter-judge correlations were taken over *several random scaling applications*, the tendency of such an average would be to approximate this 0.00 value. It has been suggested that an inter-judge correlation of +0.70 or higher constitutes sufficient agreement to permit the use of the results for analysis. Such an inter-judge correlation indicates that the average disagreement is in the order of 1.5 categories per unit-statement or assertion.[17] Considering that a scaling judge must choose between nine categories of differentiation, this coefficient suggests a respectable level of agreement between judges. If such a standard of agreement between scaling judges is not achieved, then a third and perhaps a fourth, judge may be introduced in order to strengthen the data on the basis of consensus.

The introduction of this consensus of judgments, which is derived from three or more scaling judges, provides a composite reliability. The computation of a composite reliability coefficient among several judges is justified by the possibility of correlating the mean judgments of pairs of scalers on the same universe of statements.[18] The formula for computing this composite reliability reads as follows:

$$r \text{ (composite)} = \frac{N(\text{av. inter-judge correlation})}{1 + [(N\text{-}1) \text{ av. inter-judge correlation})]},$$

in which N refers to the number of judges participating in the consensus.[19] This composite reliability will always be higher than the simple inter-judge correlation. It has been suggested that a composite reliability of +0.80 is adequate to secure the reliability of the data for analysis.[20] Assuming that three scaling judges have achieved an average inter-judge correlation of +0.65, the composite reliability for these judges would be +0.85 for the universe of statements scaled. Composite reliability may be applied if a mean of the judgments of scaling judges for each statement is used for analyzing the set of data.

The category-values derived from the scaling process are assigned as attributes to the unit-statements which have been scaled. This value is entered upon a basic data sheet or IBM card upon which other relevant information pertaining to the given assertion have been recorded. For analysis, the mean of the series of judgments on a particular unit-statement is used.

Analyzing the Scaled Data

Analysis of the data introduces the question of which sets of category-values are to be combined and what types of indices derived. The investigator will make this decision on the basis of the particular theory and corresponding set of hypotheses which have been developed.

A simple formula is suggested which will serve to determine any expression of intensity by a particular variable which has been scaled. If V represents the degree or intensity of such an expression, then:

$$V_{ij} = \frac{\Sigma\,(dc)}{N}, \text{ in which } i \text{ represents the}$$

actor involved (for example, a country or a specific decision-maker), and j refers to the time-unit for which an index is being sought.[21] The dc quantity is the category-value assigned to the descriptive-connective of the given unit-statement or assertion. Hence, this symbol represents a single measure of the intensity of the variable, while V stands for its cumulative expression in the formula. The unit-statements included in the N quantity are defined by any combination of the remaining components (that is, perceiver, perceived, and target), and by other basic information such as the date the statement originated, the type of communication media, and so on. Example: Suppose one wanted to determine the indices for Country X as a target of hostility from "time 1" through "time 5," the following simple algebraic expressions would apply:

$$H_{x1} = \frac{\Sigma (dc)_{x1}}{N_{x1}}, H_{x2} = \frac{\Sigma (dc)_{x2}}{N_{x2}},$$ and so on, in which the sub-

scripts, 1, 2, . . . 5, would represent the sequence of time-units.[22] The derived H values, as well as the corresponding N values, would most likely indicate a fluctuation over this time span. The result of the analysis would provide a sequence of indices, which permits a trend plotting of the intensity of expression by the variable hostility. Other formulas may be similarly developed, depending upon the particular information which is desired by the investigator.

Critics of the Q-Sort method have pointed out that it permits comparison only within the *one universe* which is scaled. In one sense, this observation is correct, that is, with respect to comparing general levels of intensity in two separately scaled universes of assertions, since in both cases the modal and mean expression would, by definition, be a 5.00 category-value. Hence, the analysis of two universes scaled at different times requires the establishment of a new, common universe in order to achieve comparability. This may be pursued by taking samples from scale-categories 1, 5, and 9 for both universes and scaling them jointly.[23] Once this scaling operation is completed, the statements from the two original universes may be separated and a *differential index* derived by taking a mean for each of the two samples.

In another sense, this criticism is invalid. If the movement of curves representing intensity over a series of time-units are correlated, then such variables in two separately scaled universes of statements may be compared. What is being compared in this instance is not the modal or general level of intensity, but the movement of curves which represent the intensity of variables over time. Furthermore, such criticism will not hold in the comparison of patterns (that is, matrices) of inter-relationships among a series of variables. These patterns are not determined by the modal intensity levels within the universes being compared, but by directional movement of curves from one time-unit to the next and by the comparative intensity levels of time-units within each universe.[24] In both correlation and pattern analysis, a new and common universe need not be established to make a comparative analysis of two separate conflict situations.

For a particular analysis, specific hypotheses may be developed in terms of the relationship of "adjustment activity" and the intensity of affect expressed.[25] Using the Q-Sort method of scaling, a separate measurement of relevant *action* variables (specificity and violence) and *affect* variables (hostility and frustration) will allow a correlation of trends over a shared time span. For example: The hypothesis, "Violence as 'adjustment activity' is preceded by a high intensity of frustration in conflict type A," may be either confirmed or rejected by simple correlation and contingency analysis.[26] Similarly, the ratio of the intensity of negative affect (hostility and frustration) to positive affect (friendship and satisfaction) within an international crisis may be determined. This will provide a basis for inferring the balance of reward and punishment within the given conflict situation. These examples are only suggestive of what must be a very extensive "stable" of hypotheses and propositions which may be developed and tested using scaling techniques.

Q-Sort scaling enables the investigator to compare and relate over time the intensity levels of a group of variables. A comparative analysis may be pursued in two separate ways: (1) a comparison across a set of variables within the same conflict situation; and (2) a comparison across conflict situations on the basis of patterns of relationship among a set of variables. This ability to determine intensity or degree of expression by variables allows the testing of hypotheses and propositions relating to the behavior of states in international crises.

Conclusion

The Q-Sort method of scaling attempts to establish the reliability of data for analysis by achieving what might be termed "inter-subjective consistency" among a series of intelligent and perceptive judges. The primary assumption made in applying this technique is a statistical one, that is, a prescribed symmetrical distribution of scalable unit-statements. No assumptions are made in advance of scaling as to the substantive content of any particular category on the scale. This serves to establish the relative nature of the application of the Q-Sort scale, which thus does not require a rigid definition of each of its scale-categories.

A major advantage of the Q-Sort method of scaling is its economy and ease of application. The actual scaling operation can be done in a relatively short time with a minimum of scaler training. In addition, the Q-Sort emphasizes the contextual or thematic aspect of the assertion, the statement, so to speak, being judged as a whole. It also stresses the unique set of relationships within any universe of statements which is scaled. Hence, it proves useful in detecting subtle nuances of differentiation which more highly structured techniques of scaling might inadvertently overlook. Finally, it permits meaningful analysis and comparison across variables, since a common basis for detecting variation is provided by the forcing of distribution.

The Q-Sort method of scaling provides a means by which the intensity of variables which describe crises can be determined and translated into quantitative form. Thus far, it has proved useful in measuring the expression of affective variables such as hostility and frustration in the arena of world politics. Future application of the Q-Sort will serve to measure and analyze other aspects of crisis transactions among states.

2.*

Further Thoughts on the Q-Sort

In the previous section a scaling technique which has been used with some measure of success in psychological research was proposed as a valid and useful tool for comparable research problems in international relations. The question naturally arises: What types of problems in international relations are

* The major author of this section is Dina A. Zinnes, and was written while the author held the Esther Caukin Brunauer Fellowship from the American Association of University Women. The author wishes to thank Joseph Zinnes for his help and suggestions in the preparation of this section.

amenable to the use of Q-Sorting techniques? It also remains to assess the advantages and disadvantages which accrue from its application.

It is not our intention to present a history of Q-Sorting, the literature of which has been marked by lack of terminological uniformity and by often obscure technical debates.[27] However, it may be of benefit to the reader in evaluating the potential application of the Q-Sort to have a brief description of its origins. The Q-Sort is essentially a modification of the usual correlation design in which the scores of a group of people on two or more tests are correlated. The research design, in these instances, consists of correlating tests *over individuals*. The modification of this design which led to the development of the Q-Sort consisted of correlating two individuals *over* a group of *tests*. In this latter situation it was possible to compare the reactions of two particular individuals. This modification introduced a new problem. In the original research design it was permissible to correlate a group of individuals over two tests, since the scores on any one test were comparable from one individual to another; one could compare a score of 10 with a score of 50 on the same mathematics test. In the modified research design this is no longer valid. Since each test generates a different measuring unit, the scores on tests are not comparable. The Q-Sort was introduced to alleviate this difficulty. If each item on the Q-Sort is considered to be one test, then requiring a given individual to Q-Sort this set of items becomes comparable to having that individual take a series of tests. Furthermore, by having the individual Q-Sort the items in terms of a forced distribution the resulting scores on the items are then comparable. Hence, the Q-Sort, with its forced distribution, was developed to permit the calculation of a meaningful correlation between individuals over tests by insuring that the scores on the tests are comparable.[28]

The Uses of Q-Sorting

An excellent discussion of some of the uses of Q-Sort data has been provided by Jack Block. The first use he suggests is that a set of items might be Q-Sorted by two or more individuals and the results compared. In this way, the response of several subjects may be compared; for example, one subject's sort on his real self might be compared with a sort on his ideal self. Two clinicians could evaluate the same patient, or two psychologists' intuitive definition of some concept such as creativity could be compared.

A second use of Q-Sort data involves comparing Q-Sorts for one group of individuals with those for another group. For example, we might wish to compare Q-Sorts from low income negroes with those of low income whites to detect salient distinguishing characteristics of these two groups in terms of this set of items.

A third use of Q-Sort data would be to compare a Q-Sort for one or more groups with some ideal Q-Sort criterion. Thus we might have psychologists determine an ideal Q-Sort for schizophrenic patients which would then be correlated with the Q-Sorts of a group of actual schizophrenic patients. Or, as Block suggests, "we may wish to know whether individuals in one group correlate more with a criterion than do individuals in a second group."

Finally, Block points out that Q-Sort data could also be used to determine or define types or clusters of people. "Rather than grouping people on some independent basis of classification and then analyzing the characteristics of the Q-Sorts that come out of each group, we may reverse the sequence and group individuals on the basis of their Q-Sorts, then analyzing independent sources of information for the correlates of group membership."[29] This application would serve to detect basic qualities shared by groups of subjects.

Perhaps the most obvious and easiest adaptation of the Q-Sort to international relations pertains to research problems containing a psychological element. For example, we might want to compare the Q-Sorts of a group of pacifists with the Q-Sorts of a group of militarists. The Q-Sort items could be personality traits, or impressions of American foreign policy. This design is essentially Block's second suggestion; the difference is that we are studying international relations variables rather than psychological ones.

A similar use of the Q-Sort would be in conjunction with

gaming for simulation studies. We might simulate an international crisis situation as well as an international non-crisis situation. The participants could be asked to Q-Sort a set of items such as, "X is unfair," "X does not know the function of diplomacy," or "X cheats," and the crisis participants could then be compared with the non-crisis participants.

A further adaptation corresponds to Block's first suggestion. The Q-Sort could be used in international relations for the clarification of a key concept. We might construct a set of Q-Sort items which contained such statements as, "X broke off diplomatic contact with Y," "X placed an embargo on Y's trade," "X bombed Y," and "X's press charged Y with intervention." Two judges could then be asked to Q-Sort the items in terms of the degree of hostility represented by the statement. A comparison of the results, if the judges have been chosen at random, should determine the layman's usage of the concept "hostility." If, however, we chose judges with background in international law, we could reasonably argue that the results represent the degree of consensus or divergence between two authorities. If, in addition, these two judges had been selected at random from the population of those with international law background, we might even maintain that the degree of consensus was representative of the consensus in the field of international law.

Advantages and Disadvantages of the Q-Sort

The reader may wonder whether the Q-Sort could be used as a scaling technique for any situation in which some variable must be scaled along a given dimension. In other words, which types of international relations research designs are most amenable to Q-Sorting? This introduces the further question of the advantages and disadvantages of Q-Sort scaling. These questions must be answered in light of the various uses of the Q-Sort.

Clearly, the Q-Sort is inapplicable in instances in which its forced quasi-normal distribution assumption mitigates against the acquisition of data necessary to the research problem. For example, suppose that we want to describe a crisis situation in terms of the distribution of the intensity of each of several variables, such as, hostility, friendship, frustration, and satisfaction. If the intensity of each variable had been scaled on the basis of the Q-Sort, it would not be possible to make this analysis, for the distribution of each variable has already been pre-determined— it is normal. In these instances it is necessary to use a different scaling process.[30]

Now we may turn to a discussion of a series of advantages and disadvantages of the Q-Sort.

1. When Q-Sorting a set of statements is completed, the value assigned to each statement reflects its intensity in relation to that given universe of statements. Thus, by taking a smaller or larger universe, or by taking subsets of larger universes, one can determine different values for the same statement. It should be noted, of course, that each of these different values for the same statement is meaningful *in* that set within which it was scaled. For example, suppose that we had two international crises, and that we were interested in a comparison of these two crises in terms of the intensity of hostility, as it develops from the outbreak of a crisis, through its culmination. It would be a serious error to scale the intensity of hostility separately for each crisis and then attempt to make comparisons between them. If we wish to make meaningful comparative analyses between the two crises, we must pool the hostility statements from both crises and scale them together.

A scaling technique which determines relative values is useful in many types of research problems. The only disadvantage of a relative scale occurs if we wish to make generalizations in "absolute" terms. For example, we would not be able to say on the basis of our two (or more) crises that the intensity of hostility of crises begins at 4, rises to a 9, and then tapers off to a 7. On the other hand, if we have a sufficiently large sample of crises, each of which exhibited a behavior similar to that described, we could then draw the conclusion that the intensity of hostility in crises tends to be curvilinear with respect to time.

Although the Q-Sort determines relative values which are useful in various types of problems, this property is not peculiar to the Q-Sort. For example, if a judge is told to place fifty statements into nine different categories from low to high intensity without any restriction on the number of statements per category, the result will be a "relative" scale. Furthermore, the ability to expand or contract the universe of statements is transferable to other scaling techniques. Hence, if relative scale values are desired, other scaling techniqus will also produce this result.

2. Certain biases might be introduced into the scaling process if a judge were requested to place statements into nine categories without any restriction as to the number of statements per category. For example, different judges might have different sensitivities. One judge might be highly sensitive only to extreme hostility statements, while another one might be sensitive to middle range hostility intensities. Thus, there would probably be considerable disagreement between two judges on the scale value assigned to any one hostility statement, lowering the reliability of the scaling process. Since we want to draw conclusions and make generalizations about the intensity of hostility, and not about the sensitivities of a particular judge, we need a scaling technique which eliminates, to the greatest possible extent, any of these individual biases. By forcing each judge to put a predetermined number of statements in each category, we are in effect making each judge necessarily sensitive in the same way and to the same degree. Hence, this aspect of the Q-Sort increases the reliability of the judging and objectivity of the results. This objectifying process is actually a function of the forced quasi-normal distribution used by the Q-Sort. The same result would be achieved whether this forced distribution approximated a normal curve, or whether it were bi-modal or skewed.

Suppose we wish to avoid using any type of forced distribution because of our data or particular problem. Are there other techniques for acquiring this objectivity? This calls for a good measuring device, that is, a tool, like a ruler, which will produce reliable judgments. There are other such useful techniques. The most obvious solution is to provide the judge with samples of the different levels of the scale, taken from the universe of statements to be scaled.[31]

3. The forced quasi-normal distribution assumption of the

Q-Sort gives rise to an interval scale. This feature justifies certain types of statements which we would like to make about the Q-Sorted data. On the other hand, there are other assumptions which can be made. These also give rise to an interval scale, or perhaps other scales, as for example, a ratio or absolute scale.[32] If an interval scale is desired, but one wishes to circumvent the Q-Sort process, the scaling can be done using other techniques and the results transformed into a normal distribution with the use of appropriate statistics.

One difficulty of the Q-Sort is the length of time and amount of work involved. To Q-Sort statements it is usually necessary (1) to put each statement on a separate sheet of paper and (2) to mask each statement. Since a fixed number of statements are permitted in each category, it must be possible to shift statements from one category to another, should one category become filled. This is most easily done if the statements can be separated from one another. If the number of statements to be scaled is small, it is probably possible to do this "shifting around" without having each statement on a separate sheet of paper. But in most cases the number of statements will be too large. For this reason, and because each statement must be masked, the "raw data" cannot be used in its original form. If one has several thousand statements, this part of the Q-Sort process alone can consume considerable resources.

4. Certain aspects of the Q-Sort process could lower reliability of the judging. The Q-Sort requires a judge to place each of N number of statements into one of nine categories with a quota restriction for each category. With a large number of statements the discriminating abilities of a judge tend to break down, because, as Block notes, in the final analysis the judge is making pair-comparisons between all possible pairs of statements. As one progresses from smaller to larger sets of statements, the reliability of the judging process will probably decrease, thus restricting the number of items which can be scaled.

In addition, the use of a forced distribution could produce other errors in the judging process. Consider an extreme situation, in which the quota for a particular category has been reached. If the judge now finds another statement similar to those in the filled category, what is he to do with this statement? The statement must be placed elsewhere, either up or down one category, but no logical reason exists for putting it in the higher as against the lower category. In this case, the probability that two judges will make the same decision under these circumstances is low. Clearly, the more often this type of situation develops, the lower will be the reliability of the judges.

To summarize, the Q-Sort was originally designed for use in specific problems of psychological research. The Q-Sort can be applied to other research designs provided they are not affected by the shape of the distribution of variables. Whether or not the Q-Sort should be used when the forced quasi-normal distribution is not specifically necessary to their research design—although, it does not in any way distort the results—must depend upon the researcher's evaluation of its advantages and disadvantages. This is merely an admonition that the investigator carefully select his measuring technique in light of his research design.

NOTES

[1] The advantages of the "Q-Technique" in psychometrics have been demonstrated by William Stephenson, who provides an exposition of fundamental aspects of the technique. *The Study of Behavior: The Q-Technique and Its Methodology* (Chicago: The University of Chicago Press, 1953).

[2] The best recent exposition of the "Q-Sort Method" is provided by Jack Block, who discusses its application in psychology. *The Q-Sort Method in Personality Assessment and Psychiatric Research* (Springfield, Ill.: Charles C Thomas, 1961).

[3] Several variables which have been scaled in the work of the Stanford Studies in International Conflict and Integration are hostility, frustration, satisfaction, friendship, specificity, change of status quo, general affect, and violence.

[4] For instance, see Charles E. Osgood, Sol Saporta, and Jum C. Nunnally, "Evaluative Assertion Analysis," *Litera*, 3 (1956), 47-102; and, its application in Ole R. Holsti, "The Belief System and National Images: A Case Study," *The Journal of Conflict Resolution*, 6 (1962), 244-52. However, a technique for circumventing this difficulty is presented in the evaluative assertion chapter of this handbook.

[5] What is here described as the *descriptive-connective* includes the

elements of verb-connector, common meaning evaluator, or incorporated modifier which are discussed later in this handbook. The descriptive-connective would indicate three basic types of assertions: (1) the verb form, "X attacks Y"; (2) the adjective form, "The aggressive X," which may be converted into "X is aggressive"; and, (3) the predicate adjective form, "X is mobilizing." Each of these types of assertions must be coded and treated as distinct scalable unit-statements.

6 Various simple and compound forms of the verb "to be," for example, "is," "may be," "could be," "must be," and so on, would be differentiated during the actual scaling operation; they would not be treated specifically during the coding or preparation stage of research.

7 Some problems arise with the treatment of *negatives* which must be solved in the preparation or coding stage of analysis prior to actual scaling.

8 The function of the adverbial construction would be simply to give force or intensity to the assertion and would not permit a separate classification.

9 Quinn McNemar, *Psychological Statistics* (2d ed.; New York: John Wiley & Sons, Inc., 1955), pp. 33-36.

10 For example, with respect to the "usual symmetrical bell shaped distribution" or normal curve, a standard deviation of plus and minus 1.00 from the mean accounts for about 68% of the distribution. *Ibid.*, p. 26. However, in the Q-Sort system of scaling, the same degree of deviation from the mean would account for a significantly lower proportion of the distribution of unit-statements.

11 The term "absolute criteria" signifies the establishing of precise and inflexible rules for inclusion or exclusion within each category of differentiation. On the basis of an absolute system, if we assume a nine category scale, a total universe, of say 100 statements, might conceivably be placed within only three of the nine available categories. Accordingly, this type of system would not serve to detect subtle, but still meaningful, discriminations within the universe of statements being scaled. The Q-Sort method solves this problem by requiring that a certain number of statements be placed in all categories.

12 A justification for the employment of a forced distribution in scaling, and a discussion of the problem of the effects of personal idiosyncrasies on scaling judgments is provided by Block, *op. cit.*, pp. 71-79.

13 A cogent discussion of what constitutes acceptable procedure in the preparation of scaling judges is provided by William C. Schultz, in his "On Categorizing Qualitative Data in Content Analysis," *Public Opinion Quarterly*, 22 (1858-1959), 514-515.

14 Another procedure which may prove useful is the system of pro-

gressive fractionization into groups of three. Once the initial three piles are determined, then each of these may be broken down into three *sub*-piles, which provides the nine categories.

15 Block, *op. cit.*, p. 101.

16 Verbally, this computation may be stated as follows: Take the difference between categories 1 and 9, 2 and 8, and so on; square each of the resulting figures independently; multiply by the number of unit-statements prescribed for each of these pairs of categories; and then total the results.

17 Block, *op. cit.*, pp. 92-94, 102-103. This standard was first recommended by Dr. Thomas W. Milburn, social psychologist at the U. S. Naval Ordnance Test Station, China Lake, California, and later affirmed by Dr. Block, Department of Psychology, University of California, Berkeley, California.

18 "The kind of reliability meant here is the correspondence to be expected when this consensus (or average) score is correlated with a consensus (or average) derived from *an equivalent set of judges.* That is, if we were to go to the trouble of gathering judgments from another set of judges sampled from the same judge population, derive a second consensus evaluation, and correlate this second consensus evaluation with the consensus evaluation derived from the first set of judges, the resulting correlation would be the reliability co-efficient we speak of here." *Ibid.*, p. 37.

19 *Ibid.*

20 This level of composite reliability as a standard was recommended by Dr. Block. "At the same time, because our chosen score is an average, simple psychometric logic argues quite convincingly that the consensus will cumulate validity disproportionately more rapidly than it will cumulate error. Idiosyncracies of observers, inattentions, and other observer flaws can be expected, in the main, to cancel each other and to let through the stubborn truth. The expectation of higher validity in the consensus is supported empirically almost universally in the research instances where the matter has been investigated." *Ibid.*, p. 38.

21 Since the distribution in the Q-Sort method of scaling is symmetrical, it is clear that the value of V for all countries included in the analysis from "time 1" through "time n," that is, for the total universe of unit-statements being scaled, must be 5.00 by definition. In such a situation, the N value in the formula would be equivalent to the total universe which is scaled.

22 Verbally, this computation may be stated in the following manner: Find all the unit-statements involving the variable hostility with Country X as target during "time 1," total the accumulation of category-values for such a class of unit-statements, and divide by the number of assertions which are included. The result is a set of

indices which may be plotted as a trend representing the variable hostility for Country X as the target.

[23] This technique for comparison of separately scaled universes of unit-statements or assertions was suggested by Dr. Block to the Stanford Studies in International Conflict and Integration at a seminar on May 12, 1962.

[24] In this connection, see the section on functional distance and pattern analysis below in this handbook.

[25] For an elaboration of a theory relating to the relationship between "adjustment activity" and levels of affective expression, see Appendix A of this handbook.

[26] Here the term "conflict type" is used to suggest that a typology of conflict situations may be developed which would be based upon specified relationships between a set of action and a set of affect variables. Two generic types may be defined, in the broadest sense, *positive affect—negative action*, and, *negative affect—positive action*.

[27] For an excellent history of Q-Sorting, see O. Hobart Mowrer, "Q-Technique—Description, History, and Critique," in O. Hobart Mowrer, *Psychotherapy Theory and Research* (New York: Ronald Press Co., 1953). Additional discussions may be found in Lee J. Cronbach, "Correlation between Persons as a Research Tool," in Mowrer, *op cit.;* William Stephenson, *The Study of Behavior*, Chicago: University of Chicago Press, 1953; Jack Block, *The Q-Sort Method in Personality Assessment and Psychiatric Research* (Springfield, Illinois: Charles C Thomas, 1961); and Block, "A Comparison of the Forced and Unforced Q-Sorting Procedure," *Educational and Psychological Measurement*, 16 (1956), 481-493.

[28] It has been pointed out to this author, however, that a forced distribution is unnecessary if a sorting process is used. If an individual sorts the Q-sort items along the same scale regardless of the distribution employed, it can be reasonably argued that the scores for the items do have a meaning relative to one another, since they were sorted by the same individual along the same dimension.

[29] Block, *The Q-Sort Method in Personality Assessment and Psychiatric Research*, p. 107.

[30] See Section I of this chapter for another technique by which to circumvent this difficulty.

[31] See the following chapter for the discussion of such a technique.

[32] For a discussion of scale types see Patrick Suppes and Joseph L. Zinnes, "Basic Measurement Theory," R. R. Bush, E. Galanter and R. D. Luce (eds.), *Handbook of Mathematical Psychology,* in press.

CHAPTER V*   "PAIR COMPARISON" SCALING IN INTERNATIONAL RELATIONS

We have shown that for some research problems the Q-Sort is not an appropriate scaling technique. Suppose that we have such a "non-Q-Sort" problem which requires the scaling of variables. What other techniques are available? One alternative is to be found in Chapter VI. Another is described here.

Requirements for Scaling International Relations Variables

For want of a better designation we shall label this scaling procedure "pair-comparison scaling." Strictly speaking, pair-comparison scaling is a misnomer and could cause unfortunate misunderstanding. We simply suggest this name out of the need to give the technique an identifying label. A study of the details of pair comparison scaling will quickly show that this method of scaling does *not* imply that pair comparison judgments are made on the entire set of statements to be scaled. Pair-comparisons are used only with a small sample, selected randomly from the universe to be scaled. Before describing the details of this technique let us consider the rationale that led to its development.

Most research problems in international relations are concerned with non-personality variables, that is, variables which do not manifest differences among individuals. Thus the type of scaling procedure required will be one in which a judge is used to scale the relevant items. In these problems the reliability of the scaling process becomes critical. We are not concerned here with differences in characteristics between judges. Rather, we are concerned with the differences in the way in which they judge statements, as a measure of agreement between them. If judges are randomly selected, we may assume that differences

---

* The major author of this chapter is Dina A. Zinnes.

of the former type are minor in magnitude and can be ignored. We can, moreover, test the validity of our assumption at any stage in the scaling process. This is known as testing for the reliability of the scaling. Two or more judges scale a set of items and then compare their results; using the appropriate formula we can then measure the magnitude of their differences. If the differences between the judges remain within certain boundary limits we feel justified in assuming that the judges are making their judgments objectively, and that the scaling is reliable.

A difficulty occurs when it is found that judges are not producing reliable results. The question then arises: what is the cause of the unreliability? There are at least two main components of low reliability.

The first lies in the differences between one individual and another; the second lies in the lack of consistency in one individual's orientation to the items being scaled. We have already discussed the first component, but perhaps the second requires further explanation. This second instance will occur, for example, if the judge does not have a clear concept of the variable which he is judging, thus changing, in the process of scaling, from one definition of the variable to another. In that case, the judge is scaling a multidimensional variable along a single dimension. Obviously, then, there will be a lack of consistency in the results of the scaled items. A scaled value of three for one item may not be comparable to a three for another item because the two items were scaled on different dimensions. It is thus necessary to have some technique built into the scaling procedure which will (1) eliminate individual biases and (2) expose inconsistencies within a judge's scaling.

Let us consider now the scaling process to be suggested. Recall the scaling procedure used in the Q-Sort. The judge is requested to place each of a set of items into one of 9 categories such that the resulting distribution over the nine categories is quasi-normal. Since the principal objection to the Q-Sort was this use of the forced distribution, let us continue to use the scaling procedure but simply remove the forced distribution restriction. The judge now evaluates the intensity of the item and assigns it to a category, but there is no limit on the number of items that can be placed in any one category. We thus have a new type of scale—one which is applicable to those problems which cannot utilize the Q-Sort. But while we have gained in one respect, it could be argued that we have lost in another. For it will be recalled that under the restriction of a forced normal distribution (or under any forced distribution) the judges tend to scale with the same bias. Thus, our new scaling technique requires additional attributes.

It should be noted, however, that the Q-Sort made no provision for exposing inconsistency within any one judge's scaling. Computing a reliability score between one judge's scaling of a set of items on two different occasions will not necessarily produce this result. The judge may scale inconsistently on both occasions. On the other hand, the judge may scale consistently on both occasions, but his reliability may still be low in relation to other judges. Thus, a reliability coefficient is not a sufficient measure for exposing inconsistency in scaling.

The technique we suggest is the use of pair-comparison judgments. This device, coupled with the simple scaling procedure of placing items on a rank order basis into one of nine categories, will solve the difficulties that have been discussed in connection with the Q-Sort. It will provide a scaling technique applicable to "non-Q-Sort" problems without sacrificing reliability. In addition, it will expose inconsistencies within one judge's scaling.

Pair-Comparison Scaling

Pair-comparison scaling can perhaps best be understood through use of an illustrative case. Assume that we have a universe of 2,000 statements of hostility which must be scaled for intensity of expression. We select eighteen statements at random from this set and copy them on a sheet of paper, giving each statement an identifying number. Next, on a separate sheet of paper we list all possible pairs of statements. However, this list will not include pairs consisting of the same item twice: it will not include 1-1 or 2-2, and the same pair will not be listed twice even though the order of the identifying number has been reversed. For example, 1-2 and 2-1 do not constitute two distinct pairs. Thus if we had selected only four statements we would have the following list.

$$1\text{-}2$$
$$1\text{-}3$$
$$1\text{-}4$$
$$2\text{-}3$$
$$2\text{-}4$$
$$3\text{-}4$$

The formula to compute the number of pairs generated by n number of statements is:

$$\frac{n(n\text{-}1)}{2}$$. Hence, for eighteen statements

we will have

$$\frac{18(18\text{-}1)}{2} = 153 \text{ pairs.}$$

A pair-comparison judgment involves the following steps. Each pair is considered separately and the question is asked: which statement of this pair represents (in our example) the most intense expression of hostility? When the decision is made the "winner," or most hostile statement, receives one "vote." This "vote" is recorded on the listing of pairs by noting the number of the "winner." This procedure is then followed for every pair. Thus, with the above four statements we might have the following set of "winners":

statement pairs	"winner"
1-2	1
1-3	1
1-4	4
2-3	2
2-4	4
3-4	4

We now tally these votes for each statement by counting the number of 1's, 2's, 3's and 4's in the winner column. With the four statements the results are:

statement	votes
1	2
2	1
3	0
4	3

At this point let us return to the two difficulties which this use of pair comparison judgments is intended to solve. Consider the second of the two difficulties—exposing the inconsistency of a judge's scaling. When the number of votes for each statement has been computed, it is possible to determine the consistency of the scaling. If the variable was scaled along one dimension—that is, if the judge has consistently scaled every item using the same definition of the variable—then the votes of the statements will hierarchically order the set of statements. In other words, we should be able to rank order the statements on the basis of these "votes," with few, if any, ties occurring between two or more statements. With our example of four statements we see that the judge was perfectly consistent in his scaling; there are no ties between any pair of statements and it is possible to rank order the statements from most to least intense on the basis of the number of votes.

statement	Number of votes
4	3
1	2
2	1
3	0

With a sample as large as 18 statements it is reasonable to conclude that the judge is sufficiently consistent even should as many as three ties occur.

We have contended that obtaining an inadmissibly large number of ties leads to the conclusion that the judge is not scaling undimensionally or consistently. However, this conclusion is only tenable if we initially assume that the items being scaled are discriminable. If we have a set of items which are indiscriminable with respect to the variable being scaled, then ties can and will occur because of the judge's inability to determine which of two items is the greater or more intense. If the number of ties occurring lies within the permissible range, however, this can also be interpreted as an indication of the discriminability of the items.

If the reliability of two judges is found to be inadequate, the investigator is faced with the difficulty of deciding upon the source of his unreliability or inadmissible number of ties. With the use of pair-comparison judgments, however, and in light of the previous discussion, we can suggest the following procedure: seek the source of difficulty either in (1) the discriminability of the items and/or (2) multidimensional scaling. Both can probably be accomplished by inspection of the items.

Let us assume now that we have found with our sample of eighteen statements that the judge is scaling consistently. We turn then to the other difficulty which the use of pair-comparison judgments will help us solve, namely, that of inter-judge reliability. We noted above that in the Q-Sort the forced distribution contributed towards this goal. In our scaling technique we will use the results of the consistency test. For we now have a set of eighteen items hierarchically ordered (or nearly so), in terms of the intensity of their expression of hostility. It is possible then to maintain—since the statements were chosen at random from the original 2,000 statements—that each of the eighteen statements represents an example of intensity of hostility for an eighteen-point scale. If we wish to use a nine-point scale, it will be necessary to collapse this eighteen degree scale into nine. This is easily done by combining every two degrees on the larger scale; thus, degrees one and two will now become degree one for the nine-point scale, and so on.

When this combining process has been completed, there will be two examples for each level of the nine-point scale. We use this result as our "ruler" or "definition" in scaling the remaining 1,982 statements. This scaling is accomplished by the following steps. Take a statement, X, from this universe of statements and compare it with the "ruler" by asking the question: what pair of statements does Statement X most resemble in terms of the variable being scaled? The answer to this question determines the scale value of Statement X.

Before extending this scaling process to the entire set of 1,982 statements, it is necessary to compute the reliability of the judges. This can be done by taking another sample from the set of statements (this sample should not include any of the items used in the consistency test)—approximately thirty to fifty statements—and having two judges scale this sample by referring to the examples. Using the familiar reliability formulas found in any elementary statistics text, the reliability between the judges may be computed. If only one judge scales the entire set of statements, it is only necessary to demonstrate that his results are reliable over time. Hence, in this instance the reliability must be computed between the judge's scaling of the same set of items at two different times. If more than one judge is to be used, the reliability between judges must be computed. When the reliability has reached the required level, the scaling procedure can then be extended to the entire set of statements. (The original eighteen statements acquire the scale value resulting when the eighteen point scale was collapsed.).

Collapsing the eighteen-point scale to nine categories produced two examples for each level of the nine-point scale. However, it may be desirable to have more than just two examples per level. In this case it is suggested that a second sample of eighteen statements be taken from the remaining 1,982 statements and a second consistency test made. Again, the results of this test can be collapsed into a nine-point scale. The two samples should then be combined. This procedure will produce four examples for each of the nine categories.

Modifying Pair-Comparison Scaling

We have presented the details of pair-comparison scaling rather dogmatically. There are, however, several arbitrary points in the design that the reader should recognize if he wishes to make modifications to meet his own needs. First, a nine-point scale was adopted. This is obviously arbitrary since any appropriate scale can be used (this is also true for the Q-Sort). However, there is some consensus that a nine point scale represents an optimal number of discriminations—a fifteen-point scale is probably too large, while a three-point scale probably does not permit sufficient gradation for many research designs. Furthermore, it is useful to have a standard scale so that, if necessary, results from one scaling situation can be compared with results from another. We will discuss this point later.

On the other hand there may be situations in which a larger

or smaller scale is desired. Are there useful methods by which one can determine the optimal scale for a set of items under such circumstances? This query returns us to our earlier discussion concerning the discriminability of items. In general it can be said that, given n number of items in our randomly chosen sample for determining consistency, if pair comparison judgments on these n items do not yield an inadmissible number of ties, then the scale can contain at least n degrees. Thus, if with our eighteen items we had obtained, say, two ties, we could use an eighteen-degree scale. This method, however, only determines the upper limit for a scale; the investigator must decide on the length of the scale within this limitation.

In determining the consistency of a judge's scaling we chose a random sample of eighteen statements from our universe of 2,000 statements. This again was an arbitrary decision. The sample used for this test can consist of any number of statements. The larger the number of statements used, however, the greater the number of permissible ties. Or, to state this somewhat differently, the larger the number of statements in the sample, the greater the probability that a perfect hierarchy resulting from the count of the votes is not due to chance. On the other hand, recalling the formula for finding the number of pairs given n number of statements, it will be seen that the greater the number of statements the greater the number of pairs generated. Hence, samples greater than 25 are not practical since the number of pairs generated—for $n = 25$, the number of pairs would be 300—and hence judgments required, exceed the endurance of any judge. The sample size for this test should therefore lie between 10 and 25. We used eighteen statements to simplify the subsequent task of collapsing the eighteen-point scale into nine degrees.

Interpretation of Pair-Comparison Scaling

Let us consider now the results of our pair comparison scaling. We have now given scale values, ranging from 1 to 9, to each of our 2,000 statements. But note that these scale values are relative values, that is, they reflect the statement's scale value relative to the entire set of 2,000 statements. This fact may not be as immediately obvious in pair-comparison scaling as it was for the Q-Sort. Since in the Q-Sort we essentially evaluated each item against every other item it was clear that the resulting scale values reflected an item's position relative to the other items. In pair comparison scaling, however, the items are being scaled relative to each other *through the medium* of our sample of 18 (or 36) statements. Since this sample was chosen randomly from the population of statements to be scaled, it is reasonable to maintain that they are representative of the entire population. Hence, when we collapse the statements to produce a nine-point scale, and then use the resulting two examples for each level to scale the remaining 1,982 statements, we will end up with relative scale values for that universe. There may be situations, however, in which "absolute," or "true," as opposed to relative, scale values are desired. For instance, we might wish to scale a variable in terms of an "ideal type." Pair comparison scaling can be easily adapted for purposes of applying an "absolute" scale. In these instances the results of the consistency test should not be used as examples for the degrees of the scale. Instead, a set of examples may be constructed in terms of the absolute or "ideal type" desired. Using this set of examples, the scaling process may be undertaken.

Other Considerations

In the description of pair-comparison scaling, masking was not discussed. Inasmuch as we are adopting the Q-Sort scaling procedure without the normal distribution, it is reasonable to ask whether, as in the Q-Sort, it is necessary to mask every statement before scaling. This still remains an open question. Whether scaling the same set of items when they are masked will produce significantly different results than when they are not masked, as yet has not been tested. It would seem, however, that biases introduced due to unmasked statements could be uncovered by computing the reliability between two or more randomly chosen judges. At this stage, the investigator must decide whether or not to mask his statement.

Before concluding, one last point requires consideration. Suppose that the pair comparison scaling technique is used as described above for a set of 2,000 statements from one crisis. These 2,000 statements would each have relative scale values. However, suppose further that this scaling had been done some time in the past and that we had subsequently scaled 2,000 statements, also on a relative basis, from another crisis. Now we wish to compare these crises. Since the scaling had been done on a relative basis, as was discussed in connection with the Q-Sort, we can not legitimately make comparisons between these two separately scaled sets.

One solution would be to combine the two sets of statements and simply rescale the entire set of 4,000, following the pair comparison procedure. There does exist a somewhat simpler technique, however, which was developed for use with the Q-Sort and which can be easily adapted to pair-comparison scaling.

A random sample of nine statements can be selected from each of the two crises, labelling those statements from one crisis with an A and those from the second crisis with a B. Next, the entire eighteen statements should be shuffled together, and numbers assigned. On a separate sheet of paper, statements from both Crisis A and B may be recorded, along with the identifying number and corresponding scale values given these statements in the original scaling process (that is, when scaled only for Crisis A or for Crisis B). For example:

1	7	3	2
2	6	4	5
7	3	5	7
8	1	9	9
11	9	13	6
	etc.		etc.

Now, the A and B labels should be used so that the only identifying label on each statement is its number. The same procedure outlined earlier should be followed, that is, the construction of all possible pairs from the eighteen statements and the making of pair comparison judgments on each pair. The resulting eighteen-point scale is collapsed into nine degrees, and scale values are assigned to the statements. In this way, the old, or original, scale values given to each of these statements may be compared with the new scaled values. This comparison will demonstrate how the old scale values must be revised if the two sets of statements are to be scaled together. For example, the comparison may show that each statement in Crisis A must be lowered by one scale value, while each statement in Crisis B must be raised by two scale values. Then, it becomes fairly simple to revise the old scale value in order to make the two crises comparable.[1]

Conclusion

In the present chapter we have presented the second of three alternative methods which may be used to measure the intensity of expression in documentary material. The rationale for suggesting an alternative to the Q-Sort technique is that the latter may not be applicable, or it may not be the most advantageous technique for all research designs. Specifically, we have proposed "pair-comparison" scaling as a technique which produces a *relative scale without a forced distribution* and which facilitates the *comparison of results* across universes of data.

NOTES

[1] This procedure obviously makes certain assumptions both in its use with the Q-Sort and in its adaptation for use with pair comparison scaling. In particular, it assumes that if statement A-3 has a higher scale value than statement A-1, then re-scaling these statements with the statements from Crisis B will not alter this relationship. That is, whatever the new scale values given statements A-3 and A-1, A-1 will retain a scale value which exceeds—or is equal to—that of A-1.

CHAPTER VI*   EVALUATIVE ASSERTION ANALYSIS

Introduction

Content analysis—which may be performed using many different techniques, depending upon the theoretical interests of the investigator—is used as a tool for research in international conflict on the premise that from the content of the decision-makers' messages, valid inference may be drawn concerning the attitudes of the speaker or writer.[1] For the type of research described in this manual, the method of content analysis must fulfill a number of requirements.

1. It must provide *valid* results.
2. It must provide *reliable* results.[2]
3. It must provide results which are capable of *quantification*.[3] A continuing study of world tension levels, for example, requires a technique which provides not only a measure of the appearance or non-appearance of certain attitudes, but also of the *intensity* of those attitudes.

One method meeting these requirements is "evaluative assertion analysis,"[4] a form of quantitative content analysis in which messages are translated into simple, three-element assertive format. Numerical values are then assigned to the constituent elements of each assertion, depending upon its direction and intensity.

Evaluative assertion analysis is not merely a technique for scaling previously coded data. Rather, it is an all-inclusive method of content analysis; as such it prescribes comprehensive rules for each step from the initial preparation of the written text through the final analysis of the processed data.

---

* The major author of this chapter is Ole R. Holsti.

This technique was designed for the study of evaluative attitudes on a "good-bad" continuum; its senior author has demonstrated elsewhere, through factor analysis of semantic differentials, that the good-bad, active-passive, and strong-weak dimensions dominate human expression.[5] The mechanics of the method, however, are suitable for analysis of any dimension defined as a continuum between polar opposites. The technique is also readily adaptable for measuring categories that are defined, as in Q-Sort scaling, as a single "more-to-less" continuum. For the study of international conflict, relevant variables, in addition to those mentioned above, include: hostility-friendship, satisfaction-frustration, strength-weakness, specificity-diffuseness, and violence-nonviolence. Any dimensions chosen for analysis must, of course, be explicitly defined.

As with all kinds of content analysis, evaluative assertion analysis rests upon certain minimal premises regarding (1) the structure of messages, and (2) the operations which can be undertaken by reasonably skilled coders with an acceptable degree of reliability. These assumptions have, however, been empirically shown to be valid.[6]

It will suffice for the purpose of this manual to outline very briefly the primary characteristics of this technique. A reader contemplating the use of evaluative assertion analysis should turn to the original source for a comprehensive description;[7] the summary below will serve as an introduction to the method and as the basis for discussing its utility in research on international conflict.

Coding and Scaling

The steps for converting unedited messages into the quantified data against which hypotheses can be tested are as follows:

1. The initial step in evaluative assertion analysis is the identification and isolation of attitude objects in relation to the variables under study.[8] Attitude objects are symbols whose evaluative meanings vary from person to person; for example, capitalism, foreign aid, United Nations, Khrushchev. Common-meaning terms are those whose evaluative meanings vary minimally; for

example, evil, honest, benevolent. In general, terms which are capitalized are attitude objects rather than common-meaning terms.

2. After attitude objects—which might include nations, policies, ideologies, decision-makers, non-national organizations, or general symbols—have been identified by the coders, they are masked with meaningless symbols. For example, the text of a Soviet note to the United States Government states that,

In recent days fascistic elements with the obvious connivance of the United States occupation authorities have carried out in the American sector of West Berlin a series of dangerous provocations against members of the honor guard of the Soviet forces.

After masking of attitude objects with nonsense symbols, the edited text would read as follows:

In recent days fascistic elements with the obvious connivance of the AX occupation authorities have carried out in the AX sector of BY a series of dangerous provocations against members of the honor guard of the CZ forces.

Note that because in the Soviet note the terms "United States" and "American" are interchangeable, both are masked with the same symbol.

3. Following these initial operations, the masked message is translated into one of two generic assertion forms:

    A. Attitude Object$_1$ (AO$_1$)/verbal connector (c)/common-meaning term (cm)

    B. Attitude Object$_1$ (AO$_1$)/verbal connector (c)/Attitude Object$_2$ (AO$_2$)

Comprehensive guides for translation of the text have been prepared, making possible the revision of the most complex sentences.[9] Thus an editorial statement in *Jen-min jih-pao* that, "The treacherous American aggressors are abetting the corrupt ruling circles of Japan," would be coded as follows:

1. Americans	are	treacherous	(form A)
2. Americans	are	aggressors	(form A)
3. Americans	are abetting	Japanese ruling circles	(form B)
4. Japanese ruling circles	are	corrupt	(form A)

The complete text is typed on a seven-column data chart:

1	2	3	4	5	6	7
Source	AO_1	c	Value column 3	cm or AO_2	Value column 5	Product column 4 x 6

values are then entered in columns 4 and 6 of the data chart. If the project involves the analysis of more than one dimension, assertions should be kept separate either by adding an additional column on the data chart in which identification of the dimension can be made, or by maintaining a separate data chart for each dimension.

4. The next step is to determine the direction or valence and intensity of the attitudes, as expressed in the verbal connector and the common-meaning term. Each of these is rated for both valence (+ or −) and intensity (1, 2, or 3). The direction of the verbal connector depends upon whether the perceived relationship is associative (+) or dissociative (−). The valence of the common-meaning term is determined by whether the expressed attitude lies on the negative or the positive side—however these are defined by the researcher—of the neutral point on the dimensional scale.[10]

Intensities for the verbal connectors and common-meaning terms are also assigned according to a comprehensive set of guides. For example, most unqualified verbs or verbal phrases in the present tense are given a value of ± 3; verbs with auxiliaries are rated ± 2; and, verbs implying only a hypothetical relationship are assigned a value of ± 1. Similarly, common-meaning terms are rated 1, 2, or 3, corresponding roughly to the categories "extremely," "moderately," and "slightly." The assigned values are then entered in columns 4 and 6 of the data chart.

5. The values for attitude objects are first determined for all assertions in form A; only after the values for attitude objects in assertions of form A have been calculated, can the evaluation for assertions in form B be made. In the previous example, assertions 1, 2, and 4 are of type A, whereas assertion 3 (Americans / are abetting / Japanese ruling circles) is in form B. The numerical

value of "Japanese ruling circles" is calculated by every assertion of type A. In assertion 4 it was stated that,

Japanese ruling circles / are / corrupt

From this and other assertions of a similar nature, (AO_1 / c / cm), that might appear in the text, it is possible to calculate the perceived evaluation of "Japanese ruling circles" (in this case a strongly negative one). That value is then inserted into assertion 3; thus because the Americans are closely associated ("are abetting") with the Japanese ruling circles, the value of "Americans" is a strongly negative one.

The reader may ask, "What if the text is composed entirely of assertions in form B, making it impossible to determine any values?" This can only occur in messages devoid of any adjectives or adjectival phrases. Thus it is difficult to imagine an extensive communication in which every assertion is of the AO_1 / c / AO_2 type.

6. The scaling of an attitude object on any dimension is the sum of its evaluation in assertions of form A and form B. In each case the value is the *product* of the second (verbal connector) and third element (common meaning term [form A] or attitude object$_2$ [form B]). For example, assertion 4 above would appear as follows on the data chart:

1	2	3	4	5	6	7
Source	AO_1	c	Value Column 3	AO_2 or cm	Value Column 5	Product Column 4 x 6
Jen-min jih-pao	Japanese ruling circles	are	+3	corrupt	−3	−9

The reason for multiplying the values in columns 4 and 6 is to assure the proper valence or direction of the final evaluation; thus the double negative (X is not bad) assertion will receive the same value as the double positive (X is good) assertion.

The final evaluation of each attitude object is calculated in three steps:

1. All values in column seven for assertions of type A are summed.

2. All values in column seven for assertions of type B are summed.

3. The total of the values derived in steps 1 and 2 is then divided by the modular sum of column 3.

The final evaluation may be expressed algebraically as,[11]

$$\text{Evaluation }_{AO_1} = \frac{\sum_{i=1}^{n} c_i cm_i + \sum_{i=1}^{n} c_i (AO_2)_i}{\sum |c| cm + \sum |c| AO_2}$$

Applications of Evaluative Assertion Analysis

The results of the completed analysis may be aggregated in a variety of ways. For some projects it might be useful to compare single documents, whereas for others the analyst may be interested in compiling totals for all documents within prescribed time periods. In other cases, it may be desirable to combine results in terms of the senders or recipients of the messages.[12] Such a decision will, of course, be dictated by the nature of the research problem.

A number of objections may be raised against evaluative assertion analysis. In the first place, the method is admittedly time consuming.[13] A second point is that the translation of the text into assertion form leads to some loss in the "flavor" of the original message.

There is some weight in both objections, but the technique has many compensating advantages. By translating all messages into assertion form, much is gained by providing a high degree of uniformity for the judges who must do the scaling. Three major sources of low reliability are (1) the ambiguity of categories, (2) confusion over the perceived roles of various attitude objects within a sentence, and (3) difficulty in assigning numerical values to complex statements. Each of these points will be considered in terms of evaluative assertion analysis.

The first problem is primarily a theoretical one and precedes the coding stage. However, a technique which reduces each sentence to its constituent elements eliminates the possibility of more than one dimension appearing in any one assertion. This may be illustrated by a typical Chinese statement during the U-2 crisis: "The Chinese people firmly support the stand of the Soviet Government in opposing United States imperialism's war provocation and its sabotage of the Summit Conference." This sentence consists of a number of attitude objects in a complex relationship. In addition, the sentence contains elements of friendship (firmly support), hostility (oppose, war provocation, sabotage), evaluation (just stand), and policy conditions (firmly support, war provocation, sabotage, opposing). The unedited text clearly poses a problem for the scaler; when coded in assertion form which separates the various elements, the difficulties are materially reduced.

Chinese people	/ firmly support	/ Soviet Government
Soviet Government's stand	/ is	/ just
Soviet Government	/ opposes	/ the United States
United States	/ is	/ imperialistic
United States	/ provokes	/ war
United States	/ sabotaged	/ Summit Conference

A second source of difficulty with many techniques, arising usually after a sentence has been masked, is the possibility of confusing the perceived roles of the various attitude objects in any sentence. In the statement cited above, for example, there are three actors—the Chinese people, the Soviet Government, and the United States—and maintaining their perceived relationship is of crucial importance. The translation of statements into assertion form minimizes the possibility of confusion because the position of each element in the assertion is always the same. The data sheets themselves impose a high degree of uniformity, being divided into columns which maintain that order throughout.

As stated elsewhere in this manual, the essential theoretical components of any statement are (1) perceiver, (2) perceived, (3) action, and (4) target. Evaluative assertion analysis is readily adaptable to such a conceptualization:

Perceiver	= Source
Perceived	= Attitude Object$_1$
Action	= Verbal Connector
Target	= Attitude Object$_2$

In addition, there is a vital fifth element, the incorporated modifiers, which may be connected to the perceiver, perceived, or target. One of the valuable characteristics of evaluative assertion analysis is that it forces a separation, for the purposes of analysis, of "action assertions" from "evaluative assertions."[14] The importance of this point can be illustrated in the statement, "The valiant X has repelled the treacherous forces of Y." Although it includes only one perceiver (author of the statement), one perceived (X), one action (has repelled), and one target (Y), the statement creates difficulties—both for the coder who must categorize it and for the scaler who must assign it a numerical value—owing to the presence of the affective elements "valiant" and "treacherous," in addition to the action element of "has repelled." But when the sentence is translated into:

1. X / has repelled / Y   (action assertion)
2. X / is / valiant   (evaluative assertion)
3. Y / is / treacherous   (evaluative assertion)

much of the difficulty, both in categorization and in assigning numerical values, is resolved. Assertion 1 can then be scaled for action dimensions such as activity-passivity, specificity-diffuseness or violence-non-violence; assertions 2 and 3 can be scaled for affective dimensions such as good-bad or hostility-friendship.

When this fifth element, the incorporated modifier, has been introduced as a separate constituent, the conversion between the theoretical framework developed in this manual and evaluative assertion analysis is complete:

Perceiver	= Source
Perceived	= Attitude Object$_1$
Action (or attributive verb)	= Verbal Connector
Target	= Attitude Object$_2$
Incorporated Modifiers	= Common-meaning terms

A third source of low reliability—difficulty over the assignment of numerical values to complex sentences—is reduced to a minimum by allowing the scaler to focus his attention first on the verbal connector and then on the common meaning term, in each case a single word or a short phrase. When all data have been processed, it is possible to do a rapid congruity check on the finished data sheets to detect any errors.[15]

Unlike forced distribution scaling techniques, evaluative assertion analysis is amenable to comparative analysis *across* as well as *within* universes of statements. For example, a project may involve scaling all Soviet statements in the month before the U-2 incident and the month after the affair as separate bodies of data, in order to test hypotheses concerning the patterns of variables. If, however, it is also desirable to compare hostility levels between the two months, this cannot be done using any forced distribution scaling technique without further rescaling of at least samples from the combined universes, because the *mean* hostility level for each month is by definition identical.[16] While this additional step is by no means an insurmountable barrier, a technique which defines the value of each value category rather rigorously beforehand bypasses some of the problems of comparative analysis.

Adaptability to Computer Analysis

A final point which may be considered is the adaptability of evaluative assertion analysis to computer analysis. Because the ideal system—a mechanical technique in which unedited text could be fed into the machine—is at least several years away from being made operational,[17] computer content analysis at present requires considerable editing. Translation into assertion form appears to be one of the methods most readily adaptable to this type of analysis.

The text can be punched directly on to IBM cards in assertion form, dictionaries for the various desired dimensions can be compiled in advance, and values may be assigned to both verbal connectors and common-meaning terms using any of the many methods available.[18] Retrieval of relevant assertions, assignment of values, and the arithmetic computations can easily be performed by the computer. Finally, the results can be aggregated in terms of the researcher's hypotheses.

Conclusion

It is almost inevitable that research into international conflict involving any extensive use of content analysis will be group research, utilizing teams of translators, coders, scalers, data recorders, programmers, analysts, and others. Because both coders and scalers are likely to be part-time and short-term employees of the research project, the rules for coding and scaling must be sufficiently comprehensive to avoid ambiguity, yet simple enough to be easily learned. For this reason a technique of content analysis such as evaluative assertion analysis—which imposes a high degree of uniformity on each of the various steps of data preparation and analysis—can be of great value. Moreover, research personnel can be rapidly trained. The increment of additional time required to use evaluative assertion analysis must be weighed against the degree of reliability and precision that is gained; in the end, however, the selection of a methodological tool must rest upon the nature of the research problem and the information which the researcher seeks to obtain from the communications to be analyzed.

NOTES

[1] Charles E. Osgood, George J. Suci, and Percy I. Tannenbaum, *The Measurement of Meaning* (Urbana: University of Illinois, 1957), p. 9. The encoding-decoding processes involving source systems, message systems, and receiver systems, and the problem of inferences about the source and receiver are discussed in many of the writings of Charles E. Osgood, including, "The Representational Model." In Ithiel de Sola Pool, (ed.) *Trends in Content Analysis* (Urbana: University of Illinois Press, 1959), pp. 34-36. The various

uses of content analysis are discussed in Dorwin P. Cartwright, "Analysis of Qualitative Material." In Leon Festinger and Daniel Katz, (eds.) *Research Methods in the Behavioral Sciences* (New York: The Dryden Press, 1953), and Bernard Berelson, *Content Analysis in Communications Research* (Glencoe: The Free Press, 1952).

2 Validity and reliability have been defined in Chapter III above. More extensive discussions of validity and reliability may be found in Helen Peak, "Problems of Objective Observation," in Festinger and Katz, *op. cit.*, pp. 283-296, and Roger W. Heyns and Alvin F. Zander, "Observation of Group Behavior," in *ibid.*, pp. 408-13.

3 *Qualitative* content analysis is concerned with the presence or non-presence of attributes in messages. *Quantitative* content analysis may be of two kinds: (1) techniques which depend upon *frequency* distribution as the basis for making inferences, and (2) methods which seek to measure *intensity* independently of frequency. Evaluative assertion analysis is of the latter type; although the results may be subjected to frequency analysis, the investigator, whose sole interest is in the *frequency* rather than *intensity* of designated dimensions, will probably turn to other, somewhat less time-consuming techniques. Further discussions of these questions may be found in Alexander L. George, "Quantitative and Qualitative Approaches to Content Analysis," in Ithiel de Sola Pool, (ed.) *op. cit.*, pp. 7-32, and Ithiel de Sola Pool, "Trends in Content Analysis Today: A Summary," *ibid.*, pp. 189-234.

4 The most complete guide to this technique is Charles E. Osgood, Sol Saporta, and Jum C. Nunnally, "Evaluative Assertion Analysis," *Litera*, 3 (1956), 47-102. A briefer, and more readily accessible, summary may be found in Osgood, "The Representational Model," *op. cit.*, pp. 41-54. The present brief description of the various steps in evaluative assertion analysis is derived from these sources.

5 Osgood, Suci, and Tannenbaum, *op. cit.*, pp. 50-51, 72-73.

6 Osgood, Saporta, and Nunnally, *op. cit.*, pp. 47-48.

7 See note 4 above for references.

8 Osgood, Saporta, and Nunnally, *op. cit.*, p. 49.

9 Comprehensive guides for translation of text into assertion form and for assigning values to c's and cm's may be found in *ibid.*, pp. 59-80 and 80-89 respectively.

10 The continuum has a middle point of zero. Any one statement, however, with an evaluative product of zero should not be coded. For example, the assertion "Kennedy is a man," has a value of zero on a friendship-hostility scale. Thus the statement is not coded.

11 This formula gives a "weighted" evaluation (see Osgood, Saporta, and Nunnally, *op. cit.*, p. 92). For research of this kind described in this manual, an unweighted evaluation (in which each assertion is

given equal value), may be more desirable. In this case, the following formula may be used:

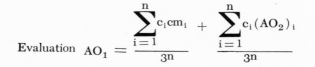

$$\text{Evaluation } AO_1 = \frac{\displaystyle\sum_{i=1}^{n} c_i cm_i}{3n} + \frac{\displaystyle\sum_{i=1}^{n} c_i (AO_2)_i}{3n}$$

In either case, final evaluations fall within a range of $+3$ to -3. The rationale for using the unweighted evaluation formula is discussed in Ole R. Holsti, "The Belief System and National Images: John Foster Dulles and the Soviet Union," Ph.D. Dissertation: Stanford University, 1962, Appendix A.

[12] Examples of the various uses of evaluative assertion analysis may be found in *ibid.*, and Ole R. Holsti, "The Belief System and National Images: A Case Study," *The Journal of Conflict Resolution,* 6 (1962), 245-252.

[13] Coders are able to process completely about one page per hour. A short form of the method is described in Osgood, Saporta, and Nunnally, *op. cit.*, pp. 96-97. Coding speed can be increased by a factor of three without a disastrous loss of inter-coder reliability.

[14] Adjectives formed from verbs or implying an object may cause some ambiguity. Consider the assertion, "X is aggressive." This is both evaluative on a number scales (hostility, friendship, etc.) and implies action against an unspecified or general target. This point was raised by William Quandt in "The Application of the 'General Inquirer' to Content Analysis of Diplomatic Documents," Stanford Studies in International Conflict and Integration, July, 1962.

[15] Osgood, Saporta, and Nunnally, *op. cit.*, pp. 98-99.

[16] It should be noted that there are dangers inherent in the assumptions that all results are comparable. For example, even a cursory reading of Chinese Communist statements will reveal a level of affect rarely found in the more genteel diplomatic language of the nineteenth century.

[17] Philip J. Stone, Robert F. Bales, J. Zvi Namenwirth, and Daniel M. Ogilvie, "The General Inquirer," *Behavioral Science,* 7 (1962), 484-498.

[18] For example, a number of judges may be used to place words on a seven point scale ranging from the polar terms X to Y, [e.g., hostility (X)-friendship (Y)]. Average scores may then be used to assign a value to each word. For example, with a 700 word dictionary, the 100 words receiving the highest rating may be placed in the 3-category, the next 100 words in the 2-category, and so on. Other proportions than an even distribution may, of course, be used.

PART III: MODES OF ANALYSIS

CHAPTER VII*   PATTERN ANALYSIS
AND FACTOR ANALYSIS

Introduction

Earlier discussion has shown how perceptions of actors within the international system can be coded and measured for intensity of expression. Now it remains to present techniques which serve to organize and synthesize this data for convenience of interpretation. Two related modes of analysis will be considered in this chapter—functional distance and pattern analysis, and factor analysis.

Based upon indices derived from a scaling of perceptions, functional distance values serve to construct empirical models of conflict systems by relating a series of variables, such as hostility and change of status quo. These empirical models constitute what are called "patterns of variables," which reveal dimensions of the crisis situation being investigated. For illustrative purposes, a set of operational models representing the intensity of perceived "critical" and "uncritical" conflict situations are discussed. In addition, a tension index based upon quotients derived from selected dimensions is submitted, indicating how an operational model of reward-punishment, as perceived by an actor, may be constructed. Finally, a functional distance matrix is subjected to factor analysis in order to suggest "forces" which act upon the conflict system. Factor analysis is also discussed as a means by which new concepts may be derived for research on international conflict.

Collection of data would be irrelevant unless some framework for interpretation and analysis had been developed. The gap between indices based upon empirical data and general theoreti-

---

* The major author of this chapter is M. George Zaninovich.

cal formulations is bridged by operational models and definitions which make concepts amenable to mathematical treatment. This chapter is intended to span this gap between theories of conflict and measures of empirical reality.

Determining Functional Distance

The concept "functional distance" represents a measure of the relationship between two variables, such as hostility and frustration, which describe a set of phenomena.[1] For research in international relations, it affords a quantitative technique for determining the similarity of perceptions of decision-makers operating in world affairs. In addition, functional distance permits a diagrammatic representation of relationships among a set of variables. The "pattern of variables" is treated as representing an empirical model of the "perceptual world" of the state being investigated.

The application of functional distance analysis is not dependent upon a particular scaling technique.[3] However, it does require a *common differentiating scale* for determining the behavior of two or more variables, *if* these variables are to be meaningfully related in the same research project.[3] Accordingly, the application of functional distance assumes the possibility of a consistently applied system of differentiation—for example, the Q-Sort method of scaling—which has a similar or shared meaning for two or more variables.

The measure of functional distance may be viewed as the deviation of two curves from possible congruence or perfect similarity. A relationship of perfect similarity between variables is defined as a congruence or identity of two curves, which can only be attained if 0.00 is the computed functional distance; this is illustrated in Figure VII-1 by the xy mean curve. Any value for functional distance above 0.00 signifies some degree of difference between the expression of any two measurable variables.

The determination of functional distance is predicated upon two qualities which any two curves representing variables possess. The first of these two qualities suggests an index which is designated the *MVD*, that is, the mean vertical difference. The *MVD* may be defined as the index of closeness or discrepancy between two curves on the vertical plane which represents the intensity scale. The second of the two qualities is designated the *MTD*, that is, the mean transitional difference, which serves as the measure to which two curves representing variables move in the same or in opposite directions. The degree of functional distance is computed by summing the values of *MVD* and *MTD* for a relationship between two variables.

To illustrate the technique for determining functional distance, suppose a given variable, *x*, possesses a series of values, 4, 6, 3, 4, and 1, from t_1 through t_5, and another variable, *y*, has values of 3, 5, 4, 1, and 2 for the same series of time-units. This distribution of values for the two variables is set forth in Table VII-1 while these values are plotted over time in Figure VII-1.

TABLE VII-1

Time-Units
(Periods)

Variables	1		2		3		4		5
x	4		6		3		4		1
y	3		5		4		1		2
		1		2		3		4	

Transitional Points°

° "Transitional points" simply distinguish the statistical relationship between the values of any two successive time-units, and will be used for computing the value of *MTD*.

The algebraic expression which is used for determining the value of *MVD* reads as follows:

$$MVD = \frac{1}{5} \sum_{i=1}^{5} \mid x_i - y_i \mid,$$ with 1 and 5 representing the time-

units which establish the limits of this equation in terms of the above table. Accordingly, the MVD_{xy} index-value of 1.40 would be computed by summing the absolute values of the difference between *x* and *y* for each time-unit, which is 7, and dividing by 5 which represents the number of time-units.

For determining the *MTD* index-value, this algebraic expression is applied: $MTD = \frac{1}{8} \sum_{i=1}^{4} \mid d_i - \Delta_i \mid$, in which the limits of the calculation, 1 and 4, are set by the "transitional points" in the above table. In this formula, $d = x_i - x_{i+1}$, and $\Delta = y_i - y_{i+1}$; the symbol i refers to the successive periods. Accordingly, for this particular set of values the MTD_{xy} index of 1.25 for this time span is computed by these operations: (1) the calculation of the difference for both x and y separately between t_1 and t_2, t_2 and t_3, and so on; (2) the subtracting of the "$t_1 - t_2$" value for y

FIGURE VII-1*

(Transitional Points)

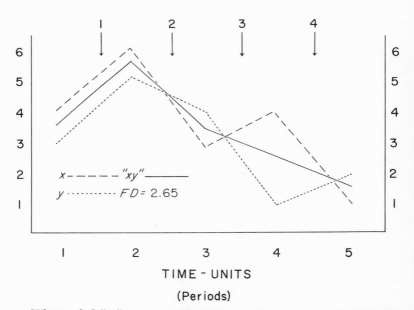

TIME - UNITS

(Periods)

*The symbol "xy" represents the $\overline{\text{curve}}$ standing in a mean position between variables x and y. *FD* simply stands for "functional distance." The functional distance between x and y would be 0.00 if both curves were congruent with the xy mean curve designated by the solid line.

from that of x, the "$t_2 - t_3$" value of y from that of x, and so on; (3) the summation of the absolute values resulting from the computation performed under operation (2) which gives a value of 10; and (4) the division of this number by 8 which represents the total number of "transitional points" for the two variables.[4] Hence, the computed functional distance value would be 2.65 beween the x and y variables.

The computed index-value representing perfect similarity between two curves would be 0.00 for combined MVD-MTD values, that is, for functional distance. The functional distance value representing perfect *dis*-similarity would be 8.00 for both of these measures. This parity of differentiating scales for MVD and MTD is achieved by the algebraic expressions submitted above. Accordingly, the greater the functional distance between variables or the higher the combined MVD-MTD value, the less the similarity in the two curves representing these variables; and, the lower such functional distance or combined MVD-MTD values, the greater such similarity. The functional distance values, thus, permit a rank-ordering and a comparability of variables with respect to their similarity or in terms of their degree of identity.

The concept "functional distance" has been defined as the degree to which curves representing two variables appear to be similar or identical, and seem to function or to move together during the crisis being investigated.[5] A *pattern of variables* will be plotted on the basis of the several functional distance values among a given series of variables.

Patterns Based Upon Functional Distance

Pattern analysis involves the plotting of relationships among a set of variables in diagram form. Once the relationship between two variables is expressed by the measure of functional distance, this one relationship may be represented as an "empirical dimension."[6] A set of such empirically derived dimensions constitutes a pattern of variables.

Accordingly, pattern analysis involves the representation of relationships among a set of variables in multi-dimensional space.

Variable pairings, each of which forms an empirical dimension, are indicative of the degree of association or dissociation of these variables in the situation analyzed. In addition, the pattern of variables provides an empirical model of the phenomenon being investigated. In this manner, State A and State B may be compared in terms of the different patterns and dimensions derived by content analysis.

For illustrative purposes, it will be convenient to continue an analysis of the earlier example. The following diagram represents the relationship between variables x and y, that is, the x-y dimension, in terms of pattern analysis:

DIAGRAM VII-1*

x———————————( )———————————y

*In this diagram, a functional distance value of 1.00 has been taken to be equivalent to one inch. The parentheses in this diagram, which are equidistant from variables x and y, represent the locus of the "xy" mean curve plotted in Figure 1.

If both variables x and y are positioned as a single point, the functional distance value of 0.00 will define their relationship. This identity signifies that the two variables tended to behave as if they were one and the same variable.[7] The more closely the two variables are located to one another, the more the phenomenon which each variable describes moves toward a *convergence* in the given situation. Hence, it follows that "distance" between variables is a measure of the association of specific phenomena in the situation being investigated.

Now it remains to apply pattern analysis to a substantive set of variables. Fictitious data will be used and two hypothetical states will be the subjects of investigation. Since coding and scaling techniques have already been discussed, we will begin with a fabricated set of functional distance-values representing the relationships among a group of variables.

Based upon the above procedures by which to determine functional distance, pairings of variables for State A are placed in rank-order in terms of the degree of convergence. This rank-ordering of similarity among variables is set forth in Table VII-2, which includes ten sets of relationships among variables.

TABLE VII-2*

Rank	Variables	Functional Distance
1	Hostility—Frustration	0.35
2	Hostility—Change of Status Quo	0.47
3	Frustration—Change of Status Quo	0.51
4	Hostility—Satisfaction	0.72
5	Friendship—Satisfaction	0.85
6	Hostility—Friendship	1.12
7	Satisfaction—Change of Status Quo	1.25
8	Friendship—Frustration	1.32
9	Frustration—Satisfaction	1.43
10	Friendship—Change of Status Quo	1.63

*For definitions of this group of variables, see the chapter on content analysis.

This set of ten relationships between variables, that is, ten dimensions, which represent the perceptions of State A is plotted in Diagram VII-2.[8] This pattern of variables is constructed on the basis of the functional distance-values which appear in Table VII-2. Accurate plotting of ten relationships on two-dimensional paper is impossible; hence, this visual representation is intended to be only suggestive of the actual numerical relationship included in the diagram.

Certain qualities of this pattern of variables immediately become apparent. For example, the dimension Fd-CSQ appears quite long when contrasted with the comparative shortness of the dimension Ho-CSQ in the pattern. In addition, the relationship of Ft-CSQ with Sa-CSQ, Fd-Ho with Fd-Ft, and so on, may be noted. The particular dimensions of interest, however, would depend upon the given set of hypotheses.

A similar application will now be undertaken for hypothetical State B. The rank-order of similarity of paired variables based upon functional distance values is provided in Table VII-3 below. The same set of relationships among variables is included as in Table VII-2; however, the length of the dimensions will vary.

Pattern   of   Variables   for   State   A

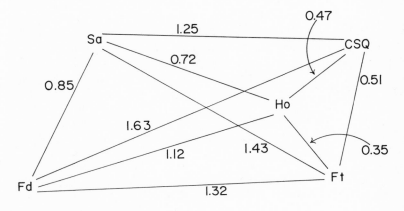

Key to Symbols :

Ho = Hostility   Sa = Satisfaction
Ft = Frustration   CSQ = Change of
Fd = Friendship   Status Quo

DIAGRAM VII-2*

*The scale used for plotting functional distance between variables is one inch for a value of 0.50. This standard can only be maintained if the pattern is limited to plotting two dimensions. Thus, some adjustments and compromises are required in order to accommodate all five variables in this diagram which includes a set of ten dimensions.

This set of ten relationships between variables, which suggest dimensions, for State B is reproduced for visual inspection and interpretation in Diagram VII-3. This pattern should be compared with the pattern of variables in Diagram VII-2 which represents State A's perceptions.

In comparing these two diagrams, the generally reverse nature of the patterns is clear. For instance, the length of the Fd-CSQ dimension in Diagram VII-2 may be compared to its relative shortness in Diagram VII-3; in addition, both the dimensions Ho-CSQ and Fd-Sa reflect this difference between the two patterns. With respect to the qualities of Diagram VII-3, the

Pattern of Variables for State B

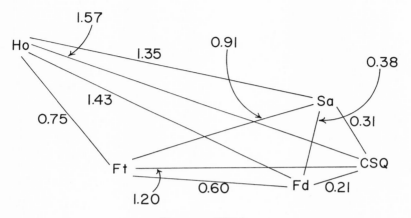

DIAGRAM VII-3

length of the dimension Ho-CSQ should be contrasted with the relative shortness of Fd-CSQ, while Ft-CSQ and Sa-CSQ should also be compared.

These patterns serve to synthesize a set of relationships between measurable variables which describe the perceptions of actors in world politics.[9] As such, they may be compared with one another, thereby providing an insight into how different states perceive the world environment. For more rigorous and

TABLE VII-3

Rank	Variables	Functional Distance
1	Friendship—Change of Status Quo	0.21
2	Satisfaction—Change of Status Quo	0.31
3	Friendship—Satisfaction	0.38
4	Friendship—Frustration	0.60
5	Hostility—Frustration	0.75
6	Satisfaction—Frustration	0.91
7	Frustration—Change of Status Quo	1.20
8	Hostility—Satisfaction	1.35
9	Hostility—Friendship	1.43
10	Hostility—Change of Status Quo	1.57

meaningful analysis, however, operational models and appropriate hypotheses must be developed.

Operational Models and Hypotheses

To derive "meaning" from these patterns of variables it is necessary (1) to develop operational models which reflect theoretical frames of reference and (2) to enumerate specific hypotheses about variables and dimensional relationships in patterns. The notion of "meaning" here simply alludes to the necessity of having an interpretive device, that is, a theory and propositions, as well as simple techniques of measurement and visual representation. The investigator is, of course, free to develop whatever models and theoretical framework serve his purpose. Only a few examples of possible operational models and hypotheses will be submitted in this chapter.

As stated above, the functional distance value determines the length of a dimension, that is, the degree of association between two variables. By treating such dimensions as attributes of a given pattern of variables, specific hypotheses and models may be developed in terms of a comparison of dimensional relationships. To speak of "dimensional relationships" is to suggest that two distinct pairs of variables, for example, Ho-CSQ and Fd-CSQ, may be related to one another as empirical dimensions of the crisis being investigated.

For illustrative purposes, an operational model will be presented and an interpretation of the above diagrams made on the basis of its specifications.[10] This model will attempt to capture the nature of what may be termed an international situation perceived by a given participant as critical. Hence, it will be designated the "critical model." Its specifications are as follows: Fd-CSQ > Ho-CSQ, Sa-CSQ > Ft-CSQ, and Fd-Sa > Ho-Ft.[11] This critical model presumes that in a time of intense crisis, hostility and frustration will be very closely positioned to change of status quo. From an interpretive standpoint, in a crisis of high intensity, anxiety ridden feelings and belligerent attitudes are expected to accompany any expressions about changing the world situation.

An inspection of Diagram VII-2 for State A suggests that it fits the critical model quite exactly. If appropriate values are substituted for the above specifications from Diagram VII-2, the assertion that State A was perceiving the world environment in critical terms may be confirmed. Thus: $1.63 > 0.47$, $1.25 > 0.51$, and $0.85 > 0.35$. If Diagram VII-3 for State B is subjected to the same type of analysis, it becomes clear that it fails to fit the criteria of the critical model. Thus: $0.21 \leq 1.57$, $0.31 \leq 1.20$, and $0.38 \leq 0.75$. In fact, Diagram VII-3 suggests a pattern of variables nearly the reverse of that found in Diagram VII-2.

Another operational model may be developed which is the theoretical opposite of the one discussed above, and which may be logically identified as the "uncritical model." The specifications of the uncritical model would read as follows: Fd-CSQ < Ho-CSQ, Sa-CSQ < Ft-CSQ, and Fd-Sa < Ho-Ft. Hence, in the uncritical model the variables friendship and satisfaction would tend to be positioned near change of status quo. Substituting appropriate functional distance values from Diagram VII-3 will confirm that State B was perceiving the world situation in uncritical terms (see above). The magnitude of the numerical values describing dimensional relationships (that is, two pairs of variables), established as relevant for these models, determines the *degree of the critical or uncritical nature* of the conflict system.

The theoretical point which is equidistant from the two ends of this critical-uncritical continuum may be defined symbolically. This symbolic definition reads as follows: Fd-CSQ = Ho-CSQ, Sa-CSQ = Ft-CSQ, and Fd-Sa = Ho-Ft, which suggests a balanced pattern of variables. In addition, a "healthy conflict system," that is, one in which all participants benefit from a heightened but not destructive level of competition, may be similarly defined. This definition is obtained by prescribing a specific range of value fluctuation for the above dimensional relationships, thus: Fd-CSQ $\doteq$ Ho-CSQ, Sa-CSQ $\doteq$ Ft-CSQ, and Fd-Sa $\doteq$ Ho-Ft, in which the symbol $\doteq$ signifies any variance from perfect equality defined as 0.20 or less. These examples illustrate how operational models, and their corresponding standards, may be developed in terms of pattern analysis and functional distance.[12]

In addition, specific hypotheses may be developed and tested which relate dimensional relationships in various crises. For example, consider these two hypotheses: (1) If Ho-CSQ > Fd-CSQ, then Ft-CSQ > Sa-CSQ and, (2) if Ho-Fd > Ho-CSQ, then Ft-Fd > Ft-CSQ. The first of these hypotheses is confirmed by inspecting Diagram VII-3, while the second is validated by looking at Diagram VII-2.[13] Their confirmation may be demonstrated simply by inserting the appropriate functional distance-values in the space designating the pair of variables forming the given dimension. Hence: In Diagram VII-3, 1.57 > 0.21 and 1.20 > 0.31 (Hypothesis 1); while, in Diagram VII-2, 1.12 > 0.47 and 1.32 > 0.51 (Hypothesis 2). In general, these sample hypotheses suggest that frustration will behave in relation to other variables in much the same way as will hostility. This type of dimensional analysis might also be undertaken for specific countries or decision-makers. For example: Assuming that two states are parties to a conflict, if for State A, Fd-CSQ > Ho-CSQ, then also for State B, Fd-CSQ > Ho-CSQ. On the basis of the above diagrams, since for State A, 1.63 > 0.47, but for State B, 0.21 ≤ 1.57, the conclusion follows that the State A-State B system of interaction does not constitute a conflict system about which to be concerned. By using the dimensions which emerge in pattern analysis, many such hypotheses may be developed relating two or more states or decision-makers under a variety of conditions.

This type of dimensional analysis may also be used to investigate other components of a crisis situation. Operationally, the *index of tension* during a crisis may be defined as a quotient derived from a specific ratio of dimensions, which reads Sa-CSQ : Ft-CSQ in terms of the above diagrams.[14] If this ratio is approximately 1:1, and hence the quotient about 1.00, then a conflict system is defined as being functional, that is, as serving to maintain the system. In order to derive a quotient value of exacty 1.00, the variables frustration and satisfaction must be equidistant from change of status quo within the given pattern of variables. If this ratio is $\frac{1}{n}$:1, where n is any value greater than 1.00, and hence the quotient less than 1.00, then the system tends in the direction of *low tension*, its extreme form representing the danger of atrophy and decay. In this case, satisfaction would be more closely positioned to change of status quo than would frustration. On the other hand, if this ratio is $1:\frac{1}{n}$, and hence the quotient greater than 1.00, then the system is in a state of *high tension* and tends toward disruptive conflict, anarchy, and destruction. In this instance, frustration would be more closely related to change of status quo than would satisfaction.

Following from this operational model, any extreme variation in either direction along this tension continuum suggests that the given conflict system is dysfunctional. For illustrative purposes, this model will be applied to the functional distance values which appear in the above diagrams. Substituting appropriate values for State A, the ratio Sa-CSQ:Ft-CSQ becomes 1.25:0.51, which results in a tension quotient of 2.45 for State A. Treating State B in a similar manner, the ratio Sa-CSQ:Ft-CSQ reveals values which give 0.31:1.20, resulting in a tension quotient of 0.26 for State B. This type of analysis presumes the validity of two psychological relationships: (1) the more an actor is frustrated by an anticipated change in the international system, the higher the tension he experiences; and, (2) the more pleased or satisfied an actor is about developing changes, the lower his particular level of tension.[15] From this example, one may conclude that State A was experiencing extremely high tension, while State B's tension level was unusually low. State A is perceiving stimuli which it interprets as punishing to itself, while State B views its incoming stimuli as being rewarding and beneficial.

Many such hypotheses and operational models may be developed and tested by applying functional distance and pattern analysis. The purpose of this discussion has been illustrative and, thus, the conclusions asserted have tended to be quite obvious and automatic. Hence, it becomes clear that State A is the belligerent power haunted by a threatening environment, while State B is the conciliatory power which tends to view the world in rather optimistic terms. However, the investigation of actual historical crises would, of course, present more difficult problems. On the other hand, empirical data should also render more subtle distinctions and more meaningful results on the basis of more complicated models and specific hypotheses.[16]

The objective of functional distance and pattern analysis is to synthesize the series of relationships among a set of variables. Each pair of variables which is related forms an empirical dimension of the conflict system being analyzed. The "distance" between the poles of such dimensions indicates the degree of association or dissociation of variables, which conveys the nature of the phenomena being measured. This technique offers the possibility of constructing empirical models of the "perceptual worlds" of participants within the international system. These empirically derived patterns of variables may be interpreted on the basis of operational models which represent theories of conflict. In addition, a set of research models may be constructed in order to operationalize and derive an index for components of international conflict such as *tension* and *crisis*. Specific hypotheses may be developed concerning the relationships between both variables and dimensions under varying crisis conditions. Similar hypothesizing may be pursued in order to compare the perceptions of two or more countries or decision-makers. Finally, the sequence of empirically derived patterns leading to violence as a mode of resolution may provide insight into the nature of developing crisis.

Patterns in Two-Factor Space

Factor analysis is based upon the assumption that, if two or more variables indicate a correlation, a third element or concept, for example, "assertiveness," may be introduced in order to explain such a common variance.[17] Hence, this technique permits an analysis to be projected to a higher level of generalization in describing observed phenomena. Factor analysis may be used for two purposes. The first use involves the reduction of voluminous and complex materials to manageable proportions by the isolation of a set of meaningful variables. [18] The second use is an interpretive one, which serves to determine which factors acting as "forces" account for the common variance of established variables. Factor analysis will be discussed mainly in terms of its interpretive capacity.

Applying factor analysis serves to determine the saliency of elements generic to international crisis—such as "power" or "rationality"—within a pattern of variables. These generic elements may be investigated by locating a pattern of variables based upon functional distance-values within a frame of reference defined by factor axes. Accordingly, a pattern of variables which describes the perceptions of decision-makers may be placed within a factorial structure for purposes of interpretation and comparison.

This application requires that functional distance be converted into correlation coefficient values. Converting functional distance values requires construction of a matrix of inter-relationships among variables which have been measured. The application of a correlation formula to either the rows or the columns of this functional distance matrix provides a basis for deriving correlation coefficient-values. This conversion of functional distance to correlation coefficient-values permits application of factor analytic techniques.

Once functional distance-values have been converted, the procedure of factor analysis involves constructing a symmetrical matrix of correlations among variables. The set of correlations included in the matrix serves to represent the nature of the perceived crisis being investigated. A variety of methods for extracting factors may be applied to this matrix of correlations, although the centroid method has proven the most practicable and is preferred. [19] The purpose is to extract from this set of correlations the factors, that is, the generic components, of perceived inter-nation conflict.

The extracting of factors serves to derive a loading or factor score for each variable in the matrix. A "loading" is a statistical measure of the degree to which a given factor (for example, Factor I) explains the behavior of a particular variable. For illustrative purposes, a set of fabricated loadings for two factors on each of several variables is set forth in Table VII-4, which represent the perceptions of hypothetical State C. These values will serve to define the nature of the perceived crisis which is reflected in a particular set of data. In addition, each factor that is derived suggests a causal element or a force in the phenomena observed, that is, it serves to explain the common variance of this set of variables.[20] A new set of explanatory concepts from phe-

TABLES VII-4

Variable	Factors	
	I	II
Hostility	.916	.225
Frustration	.938	.073
Friendship	.542	−.108
Satisfaction	.850	.053
General Affect*	.780	−.353
Specificity*	−.286	.496
Change of Status Quo	.265	.514
Violence*	−.650	.401

*For definitions of these variables, see note 8 in the chapter on content analysis.

nomena which have previously been measured may thus be derived for analysis. Hence, the factoring of a matrix of correlations places a pattern of variables within an interpretive frame of reference defined by the axes of a factorial structure. A set of factors may be considered as being parameters of crisis, that is, as providing a basic conceptual structure which is shared by measurable variables.

Having determined factor loadings, vectors which represent the set of variables may be plotted within two-factor orthogonal space. In Diagram VII-4 a visual representation of relationships among variables is provided in terms of the two factors which have been extracted. The location of each variable is defined within this two-factor space by its loading on the two factors. The relative positions of variables in this diagram for State C is similar to that which pattern analysis would provide. This diagram, however, conveys the added information of locating variables in relation to reference axes suggesting interpretive concepts.

One attribute of this factorial structure is the strength of Factor I; that is, it seems to account for the preponderance of the common variance. The variables with the highest positive scores on Factor I are general affect, satisfaction, hostility, and frustration, all of which suggest an affective component. For illustrative

State C's Perceptions in Two-Factor Space

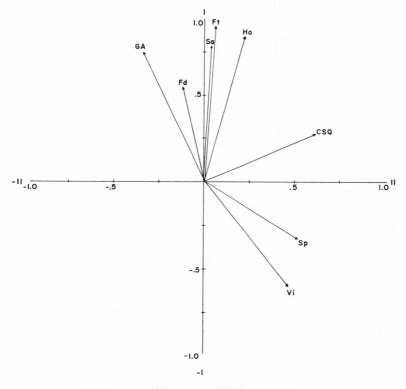

DIAGRAM VII-4

purposes, this factor will be designated as *affect;* hence, Factor I will provide a measure of the saliency of affective or emotive content in State C's perceptions.[21] On the other hand, the variables change of status quo, specificity, and violence indicate the highest positive scores on Factor II. Since these variables suggest either a concern with (change of status quo) or a mode of activity (specificity, violence), the second factor will be designated as *action.*[22] From an interpretative standpoint, this suggests that the perceptions of State C were strongly emotive but that little consideration was given to taking definite action in the conflict situation.

In order to determine the saliency of a factor within a pattern of variables, a statistical measure may be derived from factor scores. For a given matrix of correlations, a summation of squared factor scores which are positive, divided by the number of variables with such scores, should provide a measure of the saliency of the factor.[23] Accordingly, for the above set of factor scores the saliency of Factor I is .568 while that of Factor II is a less imposing .122. Assuming that these factors represent affect and action, these values indicate that affect is considerably more salient in State C's perceptions.

The major problem in this early phase of research is to identify factors generic to international crisis.[24] Preliminary work suggests that pertinent factors may be identified as *activity, power, affect,* and perhaps, *directionality*. For example, a comparably high saliency on the factors activity, power, and affect indicates a conflict system which should elicit concern. Add to this a directionality factor which stresses the "other" and we have an international crisis of considerable intensity. Additional factors which may prove relevant are *rationality, credibility, assertiveness,* and so on. At this stage of research, the determination of factors generic to international crisis suggests the application of the exploratory "first use" of factor analysis mentioned above.

Once generic factors are established, that is, the parameters of crisis have been set by means of replicable analyses, a series of specific hypotheses may be developed. These hypotheses may compare the perceptions of two or more participants in a conflict system, or of the same participant over a time period which moves toward violence. Here is a sample hypothesis: If at t_1 the ratio of Factor I to Factor II is 5:1, and event X intervenes, then at t_2 this ratio will be 1:1. In addition, hypotheses may be developed which relate the saliency of factors to specific types of events which occur. For example: If State C insults State D at an international conference, Factor I will become salient for State D; but, if State C sends troops into State D's territory, then Factor II will increase in saliency. This type of analysis indicates the possibility of predicting categories of response in international political behavior. Before this can be achieved, the association between factorial saliency and types of behavioral response must be established by empirical research.

With the analysis of a series of case studies, by which specific factors may be established as generic to international crisis, it would be possible to look for these factors in historical situations subjected to research.[25] The summation of saliency values for established factors, divided by the number of such factors, would provide an indicator of the nature and intensity of the conflict system defined by a given pattern of variables. Hence, the simple formula, $C = \frac{\mathrm{I} + \mathrm{II}}{2}$, where C represents "crisis," would be applicable. In sum: The intensity and nature of a crisis perceived by an actor within the international system is defined in terms of saliency values on specified factors established as relevant to crises by a series of replicated studies.

Exploration of the applicability of factor analysis in international relations research is still in its formative stages.[26] As yet there is little that is definite to report as to its effectiveness in this kind of investigation. Accordingly, the remarks in this section are suggestive and exploratory.

The application of factor analysis makes no presumption about the relationship between any two variables. On the contrary, it operates on the premise that the totality of relationships within a pattern of variables affords the best insight into the nature and "meaning" of the phenomenon which is being investigated. The placement of a pattern of variables within a factorial structure permits a crisis situation as viewed by actors within the conflict system to be analyzed on a new conceptual level. Factor analysis may provide a tool by which to isolate various classes of such patterns of variables and, in so doing, to convey new insights into the nature of crisis in world politics.

Conclusion

Empirical data measured by scaling techniques must be manipulated in order that perceptions of states and decision-makers may be interpreted and analyzed. Functional distance and pattern analysis constitute one such analytic tool, which helps to synthesize and organize data for interpretation. It serves to derive empirical models of conflict systems based upon perceptions of actors, and establishes the dimensions of international crises as they appear under a variety of conditions. This technique also provides a basis for developing operational models of the international system—for example, perceived as either critical or uncritical—and standards for comparing various decision-makers and states within this context. In addition, specified sets of dimensional relationships within patterns serve to operationalize basic elements of crisis, such as tension or negative affect. Finally, factor analysis, as an interpretive tool, serves to place a pattern of variables within a new conceptual structure defined by factorial axes. Such modes of analysis help to bridge the gap between theories of international conflict and measures of empirical reality.

The function of an operational model is to specify the basic ingredients of a theory of conflict, and to suggest the nature of their inter-relationships under different conditions. In addition, these operational models should translate a theory so as to make it amenable to statistical and mathematical treatment. With the future adaptation of computers to content analysis, algebraic expressions which represent operational models will be programmed directly and results derived.

NOTES

[1] A more extensive and detailed exposition of pattern analysis and functional distance has been published elsewhere. M. George Zaninovich, "Pattern Analysis of Variables Within the International System: The Sino-Soviet Example," *The Journal of Conflict Resolution,* 6 (1962), 253-268.

[2] See the section in this handbook on data preparation and measurement for different scaling techniques which may be applied.

[3] For example: If one plots and relates the height and weight of an individual over time, the application of functional distance would be meaningless, since two distinct measuring instruments are employed. Here the correlation coefficient serves the purpose of relating directional changes over time in the two measures. Should height and weight be reducible to a new commonly shared measure of variance, which may be designated the "W-H scale," then the technique of functional distance could be used in comparing the two phenomena. Thus, an expression of 5 on the "W-H scale" for

"tallness" would be equivalent and comparable to a similar scale value for the phenomenon of "heaviness."

[4] The generalized form of these two formulas would read as follows:

$$MVD = \frac{1}{n} \sum_{i=1}^{n} \mid x_i - y_i \mid,$$ where n refers to the number of

time-units in which the two variables are related; and,

$$MTD = \frac{1}{2n} \sum_{i=1}^{n} \mid d_i - \Delta_i \mid,$$

in which n represents the number of "transitional points," or $N\text{-}1$ the number of time units.

[5] Correlation coefficient formulas (for example, Spearman's Rank Order or Pearson's Product Moment) were found to be inappropriate to the task of determining "distance" between variables. These formulas only measure relationships in terms of the comparative directional movement of curves taken over time, while they suggest little with respect to the mean placement of curves on the vertical plane. In determining a statistical measure of the meaning of "distance" between variables, others have pointed up a similar inadequacy in correlation coefficient formulas. Charles E. Osgood, George J. Suci, and Sidney Tannenbaum, *The Measurement of Meaning* (Urbana, Ill.: University of Illinois Press, 1961), p. 90.

[6] The concept "dimension" will refer to two distinguishable but related elements: (1) logically, as the theoretical space in which relationships between pairs of variables may be placed; and, (2) empirically, as a synonym for the statistical relationship between any pair of variables (for example, hostility-friendship or hostility-frustration) derived by the measure of functional distance.

[7] The relationship which exists between the system discussed here and factor analysis is clear. For instance, the situation between variables defined as 0.00 on the basis of functional distance would be equivalent to the statement in factor analysis that all the common variance may be explained by the presence of one factor. Benjamin Fruchter, *Introduction to Factor Analysis* (Princeton, N.J.: D. Van Nostrand Company, Inc., 1954), p. 45.

[8] The work of Osgood, Suci, and Tannenbaum on the "semantic differential" indicates a similar attempt to plot "distance" between concepts. Their construction of multi-dimensional models, however, mainly involves work in factor analysis. Thus, the models which they construct are in terms of the relationships between factors. *Op. cit.*, p. 95.

[9] In light of Lewin's conceptualization of the "life space" of the individual, the "field" for our purposes may be viewed as the "perceptual space" of a given decision-maker operating in world affairs. Accordingly, the pattern of variables which is derived by content analysis serves to define the nature of the "perceptual space" of a particular state or decision-maker. Kurt Lewin, *Field Theory in Social Science* (ed. by Dorwin Cartwright; New York: Harper & Bros., 1951), pp. 56-59.

[10] A model may be considered a form of ideal-type construct which functions as a standard against which empirical "reality" can be contrasted. Neither the model, nor the ideal-type, is descriptive of empirical "reality," although its theoretical construction may be based upon empirical findings. The function of the ideal-type model is "the comparison with empirical reality in order to establish its divergences or similarities, to describe them with the *most unambiguously intelligible concepts,* and to understand and explain them causally. Max Weber, *The Methodology of the Social Sciences* (trans. and ed. by Edward A. Shils and Harry A. Finch; Glencoe, Ill.: The Free Press, 1949), p. 43.

[11] For operational purposes in these illustrations, a difference in value in comparing two paired variables of more than 0.20 will be considered sufficient to warrant the application of the symbol $>$ (greater than) or, if appropriate, $<$ (less than). If the value of this difference falls within a range of 0.20, then the designation $\doteq$ (is approximately equal to) will be used.

[12] What is presented here is a set of operational models which translate a theory, with no indication of what type of validator index might be appropriate. Since in this analysis the focus is upon the perceptions of actors, the validator index would probably best be taken from the behavioral level of expression. A series of validators may be derived by cataloging violent and non-violent bids and commissions which actually occur as events within a given conflict system.

[13] Since the conditional stated in Hypothesis 1 is not met in Diagram 2, Hypothesis 1 cannot be tested in that pattern of variables; the same applies for Hypothesis 2 with respect to Diagram 3. However, the reverse of each of these hypotheses may be stated anew and tested in the diagrams.

[14] The concept "tension" has been defined mathematically in Appendix A of this handbook as "the ratio of negative affect over positive affect." This relationship may be determined in terms of either frequency or intensity of expression. Symbolically, this ratio of negative to positive affect may be stated as follows: Ho + Ft:Fd + Sa. In the present chapter, the "index of tension" is defined somewhat differently. It limits itself to frustration and satisfaction and their relationship to change of status uo. This modification was necessary

for the sake of simplifying the illustration, and to accommodate the concept of tension to functional distance and pattern analysis.

[15] The proposition that non-fulfillment of goals, that is, frustration, is accompanied by high levels of tension is common in psychological literature. Lewin, *op. cit.*, pp. 9-11. Both frustration and satisfaction in this handbook have been defined in terms of feelings associated with non-fulfillment or fulfillment of goals. Hence, the relationship of these two variables to one another and to change of status quo provides an appropriate structure for determining tension.

[16] Functional distance and pattern analysis have been applied to actual empirical data concerning Sino-Soviet relations. Zaninovich, *op. cit.*

[17] Fruchter, *op. cit.*; L. L. Thurstone, *Multiple-Factor Analysis* (Chicago: The University of Chicago Press, 1947); Harry H. Harman, *Modern Factor Analysis* (Chicago: University of Chicago Press, 1960); and, C. J. Adcock, *Factorial Analysis for Non-Mathematicians* (Carlton, Victoria: Melbourne University Press, 1954).

[18] This use of factor analysis has been applied in studying the theoretical writings of scholars in the field of international relations. Thomas C. O'Sullivan, Jr., "Factor Analysis of Concepts Identified in Theoretical Writings," (Lexington, Mass.: Itek Laboratories, December 31, 1961).

[19] Fruchter, *op. cit.*, pp. 51-86.

[20] The notion that factors are *general forces* operating upon variables suggests rather interesting possibilities for theoretical construction. See O'Sullivan, *op. cit.* Especially relevant here would be the adaptation of Lewin's field theory to research in international relations. See Lewin, *op. cit.* The factors derived from the matrix of correlations for a set of variables would provide the interpretive concepts, that is, the "forces" operating upon the "field" of relationships defined by the position of variables within the pattern. Hypotheses could then be developed in terms of factors operating as "forces" in a "field" rather than simply on the basis of relationships between variables.

[21] One of the necessary steps in factor analysis is to "intuit" the nature of the factor which has been extracted by purely statistical manipulation. This practice has been one of the foci of criticism levelled at factor analysis.

[22] For the sake of simplicity, only the positive manifold of each factorial dimension will be considered in this example. This treatment will permit a discussion of action as such, and will serve to avoid the more difficult problem of its opposite, that is, passivity.

[23] This *saliency* is similar to what Harman distinguishes as "the *total contribution* of the factor F_p to the variances of all variables . . ." *Op. cit.*, p. 14.

[24] A technique by which to seek out generic factors, as well as to experiment with various definitions for extracted factors, is to apply

orthogonal factor rotation. Fruchter, *op. cit.*, pp. 106-131.

[25] The history of factor analysis in psychological testing suggests this approach. When a specific factor has been established as relevant, for example, "creativity," a set of psychological tests is developed which serves to detect this factor in any population of subjects.

[26] The following are examples of work being done in international relations: Michael J. Driver, "Conceptual Structure and Group Processes in Inter-Nation Simulation," Department of Psychology, Princeton University, 1962 (dissertation); O'Sullivan, *op. cit.;* and, current research by Harold Guetzkow, Jack Sawyer and R. J. Rummel at Northwestern under sponsorship of the National Science Foundation. Earlier applications of factor analysis to world political data include Raymond B. Cattell, H. Bruel, and H. Parker Hartman, "An Attempt at More Refined Definition of the Cultural Dimensions of Syntality in Modern Nations," *American Sociological Review* **17** (1951), 408-421.

CHAPTER VIII*   **COMPUTER CONTENT ANALYSIS**

Introduction

The general problems involved in content analysis have been discussed in Part II. This chapter will be concerned with a technique for content analyzing voluminous amounts of data. The development of a systematic theory about international conflict makes necessary replicable studies that may be compared in a variety of crisis situations. Moreover, if the type of research described in this handbook is to be used as an additional source of information in the formulation of policy, it is mandatory to use techniques which will yield results with the utmost speed and accuracy.[1]

One solution to the problem of data volume which immediately comes to mind is a research team of translaters, coders, and analysts, sufficiently large to permit the processing of a vast amount of data. In addition to the prohibitive costs, at least in terms of the average social science research budget, few research centers have access to unlimited numbers of skilled personnel who are willing to undertake the tedious tasks of coding or scaling on a permanent basis.[2]

The second, and in the long run the more feasible, alternative is to harness the computer to the task at hand. While the computer has heretofore been used primarily for operations on numerical data, there is increasing interest in its application to verbal materials. Growing out of the problems of mechanical translation of other languages into English,[3] a "user-oriented general purpose symbol manipulation programming language" —COMIT[4]—has been developed which circumvents many of the

---

* The major author of this chapter is Ole R. Holsti.

difficulties of programming such an operation. Created especially for analyzing written text with the IBM 709 and the IBM 7090, which have a core word storage of 2^{15} or 32,768 words, COMIT provides an appreciable increase in programming speed over traditional machine languages.[5]

COMIT has been adapted to a number of uses, including the content analysis of communications in sociological research. "The General Inquirer," a subsystem under the general rubric of COMIT, has been developed at the Laboratory of Social Relations at Harvard University for mechanical content analysis.[6] Some of its characteristics will be described briefly in order to suggest the possibilities that such a system offers the investigator in international conflict.

The various stages involved in preparing a research problem for computer content analysis of documentary materials are outlined in Figure VIII-1.

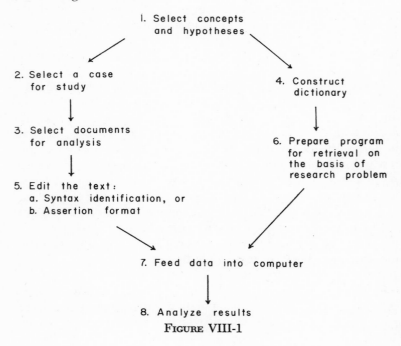

FIGURE VIII-1

Stages 4 (dictionary construction), 5 (text preparation), and 6 (program for retrieval) are the major steps involved in the use of the computer for content analysis, and will be discussed in more detail.

Dictionary Construction

The dictionary provides the vital link between the theoretical formulation of the problem and the mechanics of analysis. The dictionary is composed of the most commonly-used words in the language, plus those special terms which are of particular theoretical interest. The latter should include a separate word list for each variable, or "tag concept," with which the investigator is working. The Studies in International Conflict and Integration have found that the variables of friendship, hostility, satisfaction, frustration, power, and others are particularly useful in the study of international crisis. For each of these variables, a vocabulary is developed from standard sources such as a thesaurus or a collected word list.[7] For many kinds of research, a basic vocabulary of several thousand commonly-used words might provide an adequate list. For research in international relations, numerous additional terms, including proper names of key nations and decision-makers, will be required. Although there is no theoretical limit to the number of words in the dictionary—additional computer cores may be used—practical considerations necessitate some discrimination. Each extra core which is filled requires an additional pass through the material. If one is working with a limited number of variables, however, word lists can be quite fully developed.

One of the most convenient characteristics of the "general inquirer" is that terms unknown to the computer, that is, words which have not been included in the dictionary, will be picked up and printed out separately. Frequently used words may then be tagged for the appropriate variables and added to the dictionary.

In the initial step, then, a variable is defined in terms of a dictionary of up to several hundred words. The list for hostility, for example, might appear as follows:[8]

abandon
abhor
abolish
. . . .
. . . .
. . . .
worst
wreck
wrong

The development of adequate word lists for each research variable is the most difficult, but also the most important aspect of preparing a problem for computer analysis. The development of rigorous rules concerning the "tagging" of words, by forcing unstated assumptions into the open for critical scrutiny, serves as an important check on many theoretical aspects of the project: the unambiguous definition of categories, the precise delineation of the boundaries between concepts, and the internal logic of the research problem.

Although a comprehensive dictionary for the analysis of documentary materials is beyond the scope of this manual, a brief example will illustrate the relationship between generic language concepts, research categories, and entry words in the development of the dictionary.

Generic Language Concepts	Research Categories ("Tag Concepts")	Entry Words (Examples)
ACTORS	Decision-Makers	Kennedy DeGaulle Khrushchev
Perceiver Perceived Target	Nations	United States Soviet Union China
	Non-National Groups	Common Market Warsaw Pact United Nations

	General	Peoples Humanity Community of Nations
BEHAVIORAL PROCESSES	Policy Conditions	Alliance Invade Reciprocate
QUALITIES	Good	Valiant Honest Kind
	Bad	Cruel Corrupt Traitorous
	Strong	Mighty United Impenetrable
	Weak	Impotent Decaying Shrinking
	Active	Strike Lead Energetic
	Passive	Submit Appease Tranquil
THINGS	Components of Power	Missile Territory Fortress
ABSTRACT RELATIONS		Equal Not If
ABSTRACT PROCESSES		Begin Cause Recur

PSYCHOLOGICAL STATES	Satisfaction	Pleasure Contented Achieve
	Frustration	Despair Regret Anxious
	Friendship	Sympathize Support Affectionate
	Hostility	Despise Exploit Menace

Classification of words by part of speech may be a useful starting point in tagging the dictionary. It may serve, for example, as a rough guide for distinguishing between related cognitive and affective or evaluative categories. Often the boundary between the cognitive perception of *capability* and the evaluative perception of *power* corresponds closely to the use of nouns (division, battleship) and adjectives and adverbs (unconquerable, ineffectually) respectively. Similarly, distinctions may often be made between *policy conditions* which are perceived to be hostile or friendly (invasion, alliance) and the affective categories of *hostility* and *friendship* (despise, sympathize) on the basis of the type of word used. In general, nouns and verbs of action denote cognitive categories, whereas adjectives, adverbs, and verbs of feeling denote affective perceptions. There are, of course, many exceptions to these distinctions; thus they should be considered as a heuristic device rather than as a set of rules to be followed dogmatically.

Many entry words may have meaning for more than one variable. For this reason, every word is "tagged" for *each* relevant category. For example, the words "aggression," "achieve," "appeasement," "vacillate," and "victory," would, in terms of several variables listed above, be tagged as follows:

Entry Word	*Tag Concepts*
AGGRESSION	= bad + hostility + active + strong
ACHIEVE	= good + active + strong + satisfaction
APPEASEMENT	= weak + friendship + passive
VACILLATE	= weak + passive + frustration
VICTORY	= good + active + strong + satisfaction

Thus the product of the dictionary construction stage is a list of the most common words in the language, supplemented by those most relevant to the research problem. This complete list is then tagged for each concept.

Finally, if the research problem requires some quantification in terms of intensity and direction, the word lists for each variable may be so constructed. For example, the list of words tagged with the concept of hostility may be divided on a scale of a desired number of steps, permitting discrimination between words of extreme hostility such as "devastate" or "exterminate" and those of lesser intensity such as "criticize" or "resent."

Editing and Retrieval

After the dictionary has been constructed, the material may be subjected to various kinds of analysis, including the retrieval of all sentences which contain specified words or tag concepts. This process, essentially a form of word count, has limited utility; it may, for example, provide a rough measure of the affective content of a message, determined by the number of sentences with highly emotional words. The operation is very easy; if the computer is asked to retrieve all sentences containing the word "hostility," that word is simply punched onto the IBM card by itself. On the other hand, if the IBM card is punched with the question,

.hostility

the printout would contain all sentences with such words as "abandon," "abhor," "abolish," . . . "worst," "wreck," "wrong," these having been tagged for hostility. For other purposes it might be useful to retrieve only sentences containing words of a certain degree of hostility. If the dictionary has been constructed to discriminate the level of hostility, questions may be asked on that more selective basis.

While such limited operations may be useful for some analyses, they lack the necessary precision for many others. For example, the question above would also retrieve the sentence, "We hate war and violence," as it contains three words which are tagged for hostility. On the other hand, the sentence, "We love to follow the banner of Thor," would be picked up in both the hostility and friendship categories if the word "love" has been tagged for friendship. For this reason, it is important to take a further step in the preparation of the data by identifying the grammatical function of each word in the sentence. In addition, the text must be edited for words not included in the dictionary and reduced into self-contained "themes."

The identification of uncommon words is not difficult. For example, the word "Thor" would probably not appear in the dictionary; it is identified in brackets as (god of war), thus clarifying its meaning. Idiomatic expressions such as "paper-tigers" or "running dogs," often used by the Chinese as terms of contempt, can be similarly clarified.

A system of data preparation suitable for the analysis of political documents within the framework of the General Inquirer has been devised.[9] The system combines many features of the General Inquirer with the theory for analyzing international conflict developed in this handbook. The preparation of data involves three steps—theme isolation, word subscripting, and theme subscripting.

The basic unit of analysis for the content analysis of documents is the *theme*, which is defined as having *no more than one each* of the following elements: (1) the *perceiver*, (2) the *perceived* or agent of action, (3) the *action*, (4) the *target* of the action. While this is a concise operational definition of a theme, few statesmen form their sentences in such a direct and elementary form. Three steps must thus be taken at this stage. First, sentences containing more than one theme must be broken down into theme format. Second, parts of speech shared between two or more themes must be replaced. Finally, ambiguous words—such as "it," "they," and so on—must be provided with additional identification. For example, the sentence, "The American imperialists have perverted the peace and are preparing to attack the Socialist Camp," must be edited to read: The American imperialists have perverted the peace + (the Americans) are preparing to attack the Socialist Camp."

Word identification presents a more difficult problem. Because the investigator using content analysis is usually more interested in the relationship between key words than in their mere presence (word count), the problem of context is crucial. It is necessary to identify modifiers with referents; it is, moreover, essential to maintain the distinction between perceiver, perceived, and target. While the ideal would be a mechanical technique of solving the problem of context, the achievement of such a method is still some years in the future.

This problem has been overcome in large part, however, by a system of word identification in which subscripts are placed next to each word in the text in order to identify its function in the theme.

The rules for subscripting correspond to the basic units of the project analysis—actors and actions—rather than the conventional rules of grammar. The seven basic units, and their subscripts are:[10]

The perceiver and incorporated modifiers	/1
The perceiver other than author of the document and incorporated modifiers	/2
The perceived and incorporated modifiers	/3
The action and incorporated modifiers	/4
The object acted upon (other than an actor-target) and incorporated modifier	/5
The auxiliary verb modifier	/6
The target and incorporated modifiers	/7

The addition of secondary subscripts for any of the units permits the analyst to make more refined discriminations within each category, such as distinguishing between nations, decision-makers, and institutions.

In the sentence, "X says that the valiant Y army repelled the traitorous forces of Z," it is essential that the modifiers be properly attached to their referents, and that the correct relationship between X, Y, and Z be maintained. Although composed of the same words, the following sentences have a completely different meaning:

Z says that the traitorous X army repelled the valiant forces of Y.

Traitorous Y says that the valiant Z army repelled the forces of X.

When the sentence is coded with numerical subscripts, however, the proper relationship is clear.

The use of subscripts can be illustrated through a statement by President Kennedy:

(Kennedy/1) Premier/2 Khrushchev/2 announced that, "The Soviet Union/3 may/6 withdraw/4 the offensive/5 missiles/5 from Cuba/7."

This editing process can be done quite rapidly with a high degree (.80-.90) of reliability.

After word identification, questions may also be asked of the material with a far greater degree of discrimination. The simple question,

.hostility

will retrieve all themes containing the entry words for that variable. After numerical subscripts have been added, the question may be stated as:

1. Soviet Union/3 (perceived) .hostility/4 (action)
2. .hostility/4 (action) Soviet Union/7 (target)

The computer will now retrieve only (1) all themes in which the Soviet Union as the agent is perceived to be hostile, and (2) all themes in which the Soviet Union is perceived to be the target of hostility.

There is no theoretical limit to the number of specifications in the questions. Two practical considerations, however, suggest that overly-subtle discriminations in the retrieval program may become dysfunctional. First, the maximum number of questions which may be asked of the data in one computer pass is about one hundred; thus the increment of precision gained by asking more questions must be weighed against the added cost of computer running time. Second, if questions in the retrieval program are written with an undue degree of finesse, the resulting printout may contain so few themes for any one question that categories will have to be aggregated for the purpose of analysis. Decisions about the nature of the retrieval program must be determined, however, by the nature of the problem and the data.

The final step for text preparation is the coding of the themes themselves. Each theme is coded for the following information:

1. The time element.
   A1 Current perception
   A2 Retrospective perception
   A3 Future perception

2. The locus of perception.
   B1 Perception inside the system of the perceiver
   B2 Perception outside the system of the perceiver

3. Descriptive-indicative statement.
   C1 Observation of the environment
   C2 Interpretation
   C3 Reaction

4. Evaluative-subjunctive statement.
   D1 Observation of the environment
   D2 Interpretation
   D3 Reaction

5. Evaluative-normative statement.
   E1 Observation of the environment
   E2 Interpretation
   E3 Reaction

6. Evaluative-comparative statement.
   F1 Observation of the environment
   F2 Interpretation
   F3 Reaction

The value of theme subscripts is that they permit the analyst to code a large amount of additional information which is difficult, if not impossible, to retrieve through word subscripts alone.

The complete process of computer analysis—from editing the text through retrieval of themes—may be illustrated by performing the various operations upon one document. The original text of a Chinese Communist editorial reads:

But American imperialism has always done evil things and it has always been menacing the security of mankind by its deterrent policy and blackmailing. This is what we, the Socialist camp, and the peace-loving people of the world, absolutely cannot tolerate. Now the Socialist camp is powerful.

The 650,000,000 people of China, standing forever by the great Soviet Union, Socialist camp, and the peace-loving people of the world, will struggle to the very end to defeat the American imperialist policy of war and aggression, and to win lasting peace.

After the text has been edited and punched on IBM cards, it appears as follows:

But American/3 imperialism/3 has/4 always/4 done/4 evil/3 things/3 A2 B2 C1

it (American/3 imperialism/3) has/4 always/4 been/4 menacing/4 the security/7 of mankind/7 by its (United States/3) deterrent/3 policy/3 A2 B2 C1

it (American/3 imperialism/3) has/4 always/4 been/4 menacing/4 the security/7 of mankind/7 by blackmailing/3 A2 B2 C1

This (United States/7 policy/7) is what we, the Socialist/3 camp/3 absolutely/4 cannot/4 tolerate/4 A1 B1 C3

This (United States/7 policy/7) is what the peace-loving/3 people/3 of the world/3 absolutely/4 cannot/4 tolerate/4 A1 B2 C3

Now the Socialist/3 camp/3 is/4 powerful/3 A1 B1 C1

The 650,000,000/3 people/3 of China/3, standing/4 forever/4 by/4 the great/7 Soviet/7 Union/7 A1 B1 C1

The 650,000,000/3 people/3 of China/3, standing/4 forever/4 by/4 the Socialist/7 camp/7 A1 B1 C1

The 650,000,000/3 people/3 of China/3, standing/4 forever/4 by/4 the peace-loving/7 people/7 of the world/7 A1 B1 C1

The Chinese/3 people/3 will/6 struggle/4 to the very/4 end/4 to defeat/4 the American/7 imperialist/7 policy/7 of war/7 and aggression/7 A3 B1 C3

The Chinese/3 people/3 will/6 struggle/4 to win/4 lasting/5 peace/5 A3 B1 C3

The program then instructs the computer to retrieve all themes which contain words tagged for a particular concept. If, from the text above, the analyst wants all sentences retrieved in which (1) the United States is perceived to be hostile and in which (2) China is perceived to be friendly, the computer would print out:

1. But American imperialism has always done evil things.

   it (American imperialism) has always been menacing the security of mankind by its (United States) deterrent policy.

   it (American imperialism) has always been menacing the security of mankind by blackmailing.

2. The 650,000,000 people of China, standing forever by the great Soviet Union.

   The 650,000,000 people of China, standing forever by the Socialist camp.

   The 650,000,000 people of China, standing forever by the peace-loving people of the world.

If the dictionary has been constructed to discriminate between intensities of words, more precise questions may be asked; for example, on a three point hostility scale, the question set may be used to retrieve only sentences of a specified hostility level, or of all three levels separately.

An alternative method of dealing with the problem of context is to prepare the text into a simple, uniform format. Many of the techniques discussed elsewhere concerning "evaluative assertion analysis,"[11] appear to be ideally suited for this purpose. As in the case of numerical syntax identification, the text can readily be prepared by coders with some knowledge of language structure. The basic unit of the assertion format is somewhat more elementary than the "theme" in that objects and modifiers are separated. The two generic forms of the assertion format are:

1. Subject / verbal connector / object
2. Subject / verbal connector / incorporated subject modifier

The function of each word is then determined by its position in the assertion rather than by additional identifiers.

It is difficult to state at present whether translation into assertion form is more or less useful than numerical syntax identification. Preliminary comparisons of the two suggest that the latter may be somewhat more rapidly completed at the editing stage; on the other hand, it appears that the former, by reducing the text into a more elementary form, may lend itself more easily to quantification. In any case, these and many other decisions concerning the modification of the basic techniques are probably best left to the researcher who is familiar with his data and his specific research problem.

Conclusion

The advantages to be gained from the use of computers for content analysis are not limited to the obvious one of being able to prepare more material for analysis in a short period of time.[12] Mechanical content analysis can also be a useful tool in minimizing several problems inherent in manual coding and scaling, including those of bias, accuracy, and reliability. Another drawback of manual techniques is that the addition of research categories after the coding process is difficult. Machine analysis allows newly defined categories to be added simply by tagging relevant words for that variable; new hypotheses need not go untested because of the prohibitive costs that may be involved with recoding. Thus, computer content analysis lends to the research process a degree of flexibility which is impossible to attain by manual methods.

Not the least interesting possibility offered by the computer to the study of international conflict is that of rapidly developing a collection of case materials on various types of crises. Voluminous data on each crisis, with syntax identifying subscripts added, may be conveniently and inexpensively stored on magnetic tapes or cards. This data would then be readily available for continual testing of new hypotheses and for the comparative analysis necessary to develop a general theory. For most studies of a contemporary nature, little, if any, archival material would be available. But as such documents are declassified, they could be coded and added to the collection. It should, in fact, prove interesting to replicate, after archival materials are available, earlier studies of a crisis based on publicly-available documents.

The need for systematic investigation of international crisis—meeting the most rigorous requirements of comparability, replicability and quantification—has long been recognized. Quincy Wright has written that,

Effective research in this field [international relations] should seek to formulate general ideas in terms capable of practical application to actual incipient conflicts of the future and to test the validity of these ideas by applying them to selected conflicts of the past.[13]

We live in a world in which time between technological revolutions is measured in decades—or even years—rather than centuries; in which backward areas aspire to become modern industrial societies in a generation, not a millenium; and in which it is not clear whether the thermonuclear explosion or the population explosion is the greatest threat to peace and progress. As man has developed effective means to control the crisis in pneumonia—penicillin and other wonder drugs—so he needs more effective means to cope with international crisis.

The development of an adequate theory of international crisis through rigorous comparative analysis is an integral part of formulating "ideas in terms capable of practical application to actual incipient conflicts of the future." Harnessing the computer to that end will not, however, lessen the need for imaginative inquiry. The computer is not a substitute for creative intelligence; rather, by freeing the investigator from many of the onerous chores of research, it should enhance his opportunity to use his creativity.

NOTES

[1] There have always been two fundamental requirements for the advancement of systematic knowledge in any discipline—a general theory and tools for accurate measurement. The rapid development of chemistry from alchemy, for example, followed Mendeleev's atomic chart, which placed all the elements within one framework, and the invention of progressively more sophisticated instruments of measurement. A similar pattern is discernible in other physical sciences, and more recently, in the behavioral sciences.

[2] "Large research organizations who maintain a permanent coding

staff have found it difficult to maintain the same people over a period of years at a high level of morale. Sensitive and intelligent people who are acquainted with the concepts of social science rarely find it satisfying to make a life career of such repetitive and routine work. Rarely can such a person work full-time at such a job for more than a year or two without considerable demoralization." Dorwin P. Cartwright, "Analysis of Qualitative Material," in Leon Festinger and Daniel Katz, (eds.) *Research Methods in the Behavioral Sciences* (New York: The Dryden Press, 1953), p. 462. The selection and training of coders is covered in pp. 461-64.

3 While a discussion of mechanical translation of languages is beyond the scope of this manual, its applicability for research in international conflict is obvious. The interested reader can turn to Victor H. Yngve, "Computer Program for Translation by Machine," *Scientific American*, (Jan., 1956), pp. 20-33. Additional studies of interest in computer translation may be found in a series of working papers (P-1588; RM-2803; RM-2068; and RM-2916-PR) by Kenneth E. Harper, David G. Hays, and their associates at the RAND Corporation.

4 COMIT has been described in Victor H. Yngve, "COMIT as an IR Language," *Communications of the Association for Computing Machinery*, (Jan., 1962), pp. 19-28. For more comprehensive descriptions, see two manuals written by The Research Laboratory of Electronics and the Computation Center, *An Introduction to COMIT Programming* (Cambridge: M.I.T., 1961), and *COMIT Programmers' Reference Manual* (Cambridge: M.I.T., 1961).

5 "COMIT Seminar Workpaper" (San Jose: I.B.M., 1961).

6 Philip J. Stone, Robert F. Bales, J. Zvi Namenwirth, and Daniel M. Ogilvie, "The General Inquirer": A Computer System for Content Analysis and Retrieval Based on the Sentence as a Unit of Information," *Behavioral Science*, 7 (1962), 484-498. The discussion of the General Inquirer in this manual is derived in large part from the work of Stone and his associates. An alternative method of automatic content analysis is described in D. G. Hays, *Automatic Content Analysis: Some Entries for a Transformation Catalog*, Santa Monica: The RAND Corporation, 1960.

7 Edward L. Thorndike and Irving Lorge, *The Teacher's Word Book of 30,000 Words*, New York: Columbia University Press, 1944, is a useful reference work for this purpose.

8 This word list is derived from the work of William Quandt of the Stanford Studies in International Conflict and Integration, who has, in addition, contributed some valuable criticisms to this discussion.

9 In a concurrent project, a political dictionary of some 3600 words was developed. The complete dictionary is "tagged" for the follow-

ing dimensions: positive affect, negative affect, strength, weakness, activity and passivity.

[10] The Stone system of word identification is based on a modified grammar. The syntactic categories and their numerical subscripts are:

Subjects and incorporated modifiers	/1
Non-incorporated subject modifiers	/2
Predicate verbs	/3
Verb modifiers including all time references as to when thought is operative	/4
Object and incorporated modifiers	/5
Non-incorporated object modifiers	/6
Indirect objects and modifiers	/7
Attributive nouns	/8
Attributive verbs	/9

[11] Charles E. Osgood, Sol Saporta, and Jum C. Nunnally, "Evaluative Assertion Analysis," *Litera*, **3** (1956), 47-102.

[12] The many uses of computers in the social sciences are described in Harold Borko, (ed.), *Computer Applications in the Behavioral Sciences*, Englewood Cliffs: Prentice-Hall, 1962. Students of International relations may be particularly interested in Oliver Benson, "Simulation of International Relations and Diplomacy," pp. 574-95. Brief papers on applications of the computer may also be found as a regular feature in *Behavioral Science*.

[13] Quincy Wright, "Design for a Research Project on International Conflict and the Factors Causing Their Aggravation or Amelioration," *Western Political Quarterly*, **10** (1957), 263-75. See also the series of case studies sponsored by the European Centre of the Carnegie Endowment, the first of which is Jacques Freymond, *The Saar Conflict*, 1945-55 New York: Praeger, 1960.

The Balance of Reward and Punishment

A state tends to operate in such a way as to maximize its perceived rewards and to minimize its perceived punishments. Its behavior can be viewed as adjustment activities in the effort to achieve an optimal balance of unavoidable punishment and preferred reward. [2]

With a rise in the level of tension, adjustment activities will increase to the point at which tension begins to be reduced. Thereafter the adjustment activities will taper off as tension is lowered and will tend to cease when the cost of activity begins to contribute noticeably to the level of tension. [3] There is apt to be a level of just enough—but not too much—tension which will produce optimum functioning. Among human individuals this amount of "just enough" tension often leads to what is called effectiveness, mental health, happiness, self-realization, and, in many instances, great creativity. States, too, seem occasionally to achieve such a highly rewarding optimum. We suspect that the achievement or the maintenance of this "over-drive" level of functioning is often a powerful motivating force in both the individual and the state which becomes aware of its achievability.

At any given choice point, of course, the system may elect to accept high immediate punishment, (example: loss of millions of human lives), either because it perceives that punishment as less severe than the tension generated by the *status quo*, or because of a predicted future outcome (*e.g.*, winning the war) which will justify the initial hurtful punishment and thus give rise to strong feelings of hope.

It is widely assumed that the ultimate conscious purpose of the state is self-perpetuation, and, indeed, systematic efforts are normally made to condition the populace to accept this value and to subordinate individual interests to it. But in the final analysis, a state may feel that its status in the world community (or some other value) is paramount and that it is preferable to risk —or even to suffer—national extinction rather than to take second place. Under these circumstances we may view the negative affect generated by the perception of current national inadequacy as more deeply and immediately intolerable than the fear of possible disaster.

Using these principles we can now make some predictions about the performance of the system. Let us assume here that the state is limited to three alternatives: to increase adjustment activity; to decrease adjustment activity; or to cease adjustment activity.

Adjustment activity will rise as perceived reward or expectancy of reward increases and perceived punishment subsides—up to a critical satiation point at which activity will begin to drop with subsiding punishment. At the point at which tension disappears activity will cease.

Activity will tend to fall off as perceived rewards and perceived punishments rise steeply and more or less simultaneously. Achieving the potential outcome, however desirable, begins "to hurt too much."

Activity will rise rapidly (and "desperately") as perceived rewards or hope of reward drop and perceived punishments rise—up to a critical point at which activity will begin to drop with increasing punishment. At the point at which tension becomes unbearable, (the situation is hopeless; anything, perhaps even death, is preferable to it), activity will cease.

Activity will tend to fall off as rewards and punishments drop simultaneously. The enterprise is not worth the trouble.

Let us suppose that state A has decided upon adjustment activity through use of large-scale, violent commissions, that is, war. Again, the alternatives are limited to three: a raising of activity level; a lowering of activity level; or a cessation of activity.

We predict that the activity level of state A will rise as its forces successfully invade state B and begin to overwhelm the faltering troops of the opponent. On the other hand, as state

B's resistance collapses and victory is in sight, state A's activity will begin to fall off and will cease with achievement of the objective.

Or, suppose that A's invading forces successfully penetrate B's perimeter defenses—but at a cost of one hundred thousand lives. As A's forces continue their advance, the casualty rate rises with each mile of penetration. B's minor industrial cities are captured at a cost to A of one million lives; B's major industrial complex falls to A at a cost of ten million lives; as A advances toward B's iron, coal, petroleum, and uranium reserves, the cost in lives and resources continues to skyrocket. Under these circumstances we predict that activity will tend to fall off: the rapidly increasing punishment will soon make the rapidly rising rewards seem unfeasible.

Under different circumstances A's troops may meet heavy resistance at the border, but progressively less resistance as they push their invasion. At the same time, A perceives the reward diminishing: B's best territory lies along the border, and as A's troops advance, the countryside grows steadily less productive; the vineyards and wineries disappear; water becomes scarce; the heat increases; the settlements become more and more poverty-stricken; the women look uglier; and pestilence breaks out. Here the prediction is, of course, that the activity level will drop, and before long the invasion is likely to halt.

If, on the other hand, A's forces are stopped at the border by B's impregnable defenses and rapidly enveloped by B's highly trained and superbly equipped mobile columns, the invading forces will fight for their lives (high activity level) until exhaustion overtakes them and the situation looks hopeless. Here we detect the beginning of a crisis: can A's forces rally and perform a miracle, or will they give up, allowing their military activity to cease?

In reality, a state has a wider range of possible choices. In addition to increasing, decreasing, or ceasing a given activity, a state has the possibility of choosing from a number of alternative activities, any one of which it may undertake at an increasing or decreasing level of functioning, or any one of which it may abandon in favor of another. Within each alternative *type* of activity, then, the state confronts the possibility of many alternative *levels* of functioning. The armed forces may advance or retreat, for example, but they also may choose between advancing at a high or low operational level—or somewhere in between; or between retreating at a high or low operational level—or somewhere in between. Thus, each link in a means-end chain becomes a choice point with a number of possible alternatives—of *level* as well as of *kind*. Each of these alternatives, in turn, raises the possibility of further alternatives. In considering these various categories and ranges of alternatives, a state finds itself confronted with other states which are trying to make choices in pursuit of their own goals and interests.

The International System

History suggests that the more frequently states interact, the greater may be the probability of armed conflicts between them. But for purposes of research it is convenient to postulate that,

When two states interact over a sufficiently prolonged period of time, perhaps centuries, they tend to behave like a single system with respect to their transactions; that is, they tend to seek a maximum level of mutually rewarding activity at the lowest feasible level of punishment and to maintain a reciprocally tolerable steady state of interaction.

Within this transactive arrangement we find two states perceiving and maintaining a more or less balanced economy of reward and punishment: there is enough tension on both sides to provide optimum functioning, but not sufficient to bring about a sharp change either in category of action or in level of functioning. Under these circumstances there will be a strong probability of a continuance of the relationship within its functioning steady state. We may expect small fluctuations of reward and punishment increments—almost wholly in the non-violent categories—with a reliable but somewhat rising level of reciprocal functioning. The trend will be toward increased stabilization, regulation and integration of the system.

On this basis we may now postulate an ideal international system composed of *n* states:

When each state interacts with every other state in such a way as to seek a maximum level of mutually rewarding activity at the lowest feas-

ible level of punishment and to maintain a reciprocally tolerable steady state, there will be a tendency for the total of n interacting states to behave like a single system.

At this point there begins to emerge a situation analogous to that in which numbers of individuals pool their energies, surrender some part of their personal autonomy or sovereignty to the overriding purposes of the group, and accept functional responsibilities within the larger integration. Under these circumstances the willingness of the individual state to contribute action and to forego certain "personal" rewards in the interests of the international group will depend upon the overall satisfactions which it perceives accruing from the association—or the punishments which it foresees emerging from its own defection.

In fact, of course, no such international system has ever existed on a world-wide scale. On the other hand, individual sovereign states have frequently combined into regional systems of a more restricted scope but analogous order. The thirteen colonies, for example, combined or *integrated*—first, unsatisfactorily, under the Articles of Confederation and later under the Constitution. In both circumstances, but in different degrees, the component states put forward and subscribed to a means-end hierarchy of method and purpose in the form of an agreement or compact which restricted individual freedom of action—both for individual states and for individual persons—in the interest of certain perceptions of common reward.

For major European states of the nineteenth century, the Concert of Europe functioned as a partial international system of regional scope. Member states sought optimal reward at minimal *levels of punishment* with a preponderance of activity tending to be non-violent and negotiatory. At times the interactions moved into the violent category, but the tendency was for armed conflict to be called off as the costs for any state became too high; that is, the victor state tended to "stop fighting rather than eliminate an essential national actor."[4] Normally, the "defeated or constrained essential national actors" were allowed to re-enter the system without imposition of unduly severe punishment.

Currently the states of the world tend to function in what

Morton Kaplan has designated as a "loose bipolar system."[5] Under these circumstances, the world becomes divided, generally, into two major blocs which are coupled in what might be called a "conflict system" that is, the two parties regularly punish each other—and do not withdraw. This "conflict system" will be discussed later.

Each party, bloc, or coalition within the loose bipolar system has a leading compónent actor "which forms a pole of the system," and a hierarchy of lesser component actors. The tendency within this system is for each bloc or major party to seek maximum reward at minimum punishment—*without limits of exaction on the opposing bloc.* Inherent in the functioning of each bloc, indeed, is the assumption that even an optional reward cannot be achieved except at extreme injury to the opposing actor—including, perhaps, even his extinction.

By now it should be clear that either two individual states or two blocs of states may be construed as functioning within a coupled relationship.[6] Such a relationship is depicted in Figure A-1.

TWO   SYSTEMS   IN   COUPLED   RELATIONSHIP

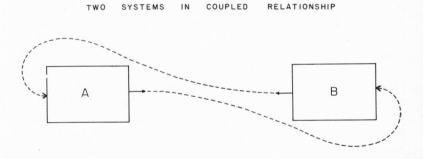

FIGURE A-1

Categories of Action

In pursuing its goals a state may choose among four broad categories of action:

violent   commission

violent   bid

— —

non - violent   commission

non - violent   bid

FIGURE A-2

A *non-violent bid* is an offer, proposal, threat, or other conditional statement or signal without implication of violence. In international relations this means category includes a wide variety of negotiations, "trial balloons," and bargaining without implication of casualty-infliction or other violence.

A *commission of non-violence* is an unconditional act, performance, or transaction without implication or consequence of casualty-taking or other violence. Clearly, a non-violent commission can be used to resolve both non-violent and violent conflicts. Among states, the non-violent means category of conflict resolution includes negotiation, good offices, arbitration, adjudication, and other procedures.

A *bid-of-violence* category includes all more or less conditional communications or signals of intent or preparatory acts—including promises or threats, whether explicit or implicit, genuine or feigned, oral, written or symbolic—which rely upon inference of casualty-taking or other force for their authority. In this sense a sudden mobilization or military alert may be as effective a threat as a written declaration. By formal declaration of war, a party asserts its intention of committing continuous violence in order to resolve its conflict with another party. To use one more example, the deterrence strategy of the United States is based on violent bids.

A *commission of violence* is an act which results in one or more casualties, that is, the loss of at least one human being by death, by capture, or by other elimination through force or the threat of force; or which violates the territorial integrity of another state by force or threat of force; or which achieves the compliance of another state by force or threat of force.

Commissions and bids of subversion may bear either violent or non-violent implications or both, depending upon the force or connotation of force involved.

A bid and commission may be viewed either in the context of the acting state's *intent*—or as the perception held by the receptor state of the actor state's intent. There may be a wide discrepancy between what the actor state intends and what the receptor state perceives it as intending. Bids and commissions may also be view—and measured—by the investigator as "objective" behavior with which the changes in perceptions and emotions of the actors can be correlated.

Any category of action undertaken by one state may appear punishing or threatening to another state and thus give rise to negative affect and tension. Generally, we would expect the negative reactions to be higher, however, when the receptor or target state perceives that it is being threatened by violent bids or, especially, violent commissions. The consequent tension, moreover, is likely to depend upon the order or level of magnitude upon which the receptor or target state perceives the actor state as operating. For example, state A and state B may perceive one another as emitting violent commissions registering on an order of magnitude scale as in Figure A-3.

Behavior of States in a Coupled Relationship

Against this background it is feasible to put forward some basic propositions about the probable behavior of two states (or two coalitions of states) in a coupled relationship.

If the perceived rewards and the perceived punishments of a coupled relationship begin to taper off, the transactions will tend to fall into the non-violent bid category—low yield, low cost verbal exchange—at a declining level of operation.

If, on the other hand, both parties perceive their relationship as yielding higher rewards with accompanying higher levels of punishment, we predict a growing proportion of bids of violence, the development of an increasingly unpleasant and unproductive relationship, and a tendency

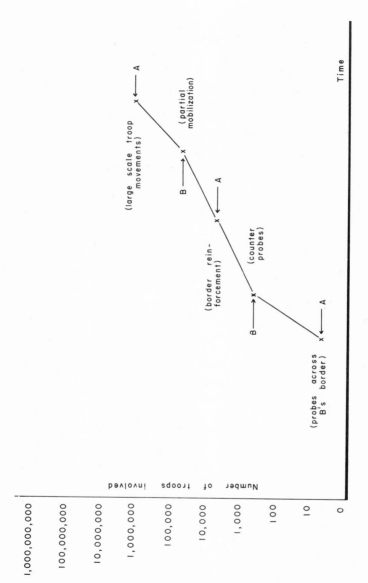

FIGURE A-3

for reciprocal transactions to drop off. (To some degree this may describe the trend of the Sino-Soviet alliance—with the rewards of the relationship, or the penalties associated with breaking it, increasing along with the rising unpleasantness.)

Clearly, this kind of "double bind" interaction can give rise to one variety of crisis: will the parties withdraw from one another (or break the relationship in some other fashion) or will they continue suffering the punishment of living together? This variety of crisis should be distinguished from another sort arising from a different reward-and-punishment interaction:

Let us now suppose that both parties in a coupled relationship perceive the rewards or hope of reward in their relationship dropping rapidly and the punishments rising steeply. Under these circumstances both parties will suffer a sharp rise in tension and tend to alter their actions from non-violent bid and commission categories in favor of violent bids. The levels of system functioning will also tend to rise.

Under these circumstances, perceiving (correctly or incorrectly) the rewards of its relationship with state B as increasingly punishing—with a consequent steep rise in tension—state A will tend to alter its activities from non-violent bids and commissions to violent bids. Its level of functioning will rise. State B will now begin to perceive A's activities as threatening or punishing to itself and will feel rising tension. In efforts to reduce this discomfort, B will begin altering its actions from the non-violent commission and bid categories to the category of violent bid. B's level of functioning will rise. These activity changes of B will be interpreted by A as confirming earlier perceptions of tension—followed by an increase in violent bid emissions and a continuing rise in the level of functioning.

The coupled relationship now has three main possibilities of immediate outcome: withdrawal; partial stabilization as a "conflict system"; or a runaway escalation of increasing tension and reciprocal punishment.

If circumstances permit, the two states may terminate their transactions and withdraw from one another, seeking relief in mutual isolation. By maintaining relations, however, each state has the possibility—to one degree or another—of punishing or threatening to punish the behavior of the other, thereby seeming to maintain some element of containment, deterrence, or other control or constraint. In other words, the perceived punishments (or possible punishments) of dissolving the relationship may appear to be even more risky than maintaining it—however unpleasant and reciprocally hurtful the transactions. Although the origins are different, this kind of relationship bears similarities to the rising punishment-rising reward situation described above.

Such a conflict system may achieve a kind of equilibrium or steady state in which the two parties continue punishing each other, but the tension and the level of violent commissions are kept within limits. More specifically, this arrangement suggests that as the negative affect reaches a certain high level—accompanied by high levels of violent bids and the beginnings of violent commission—the punishment inherent in continuing the trend are perceived as too great, and both sides seek a reduction in tension through more moderate behavior. As the tension is reduced and becomes more bearable, however, the tension of the basic perceived incompatibilities of the two states begins to rise again—with consequent rises in violent bids and exploratory violent commissions. The basic desire of each party may involve elimination of the opponent, but the cost of extinguishing him might appear too high. The cold war can be perceived as essentially a conflict system of this kind, an uneasy equilibrium or steady state of reciprocal punishment within limits.

A conflict system almost always faces the possibility of a runaway or rapid escalation, especially in the upper reaches of a phase when perceptions of threat and rising tension are approaching a threshold point: *where the tension appears so intolerable that even the risk of self-destruction is preferable to it.*

Under these circumstances both A and B perceive reward as dropping rapidly and punishments as rising acutely (with a consequent intolerable tension). The pressures are strong for a shift from non-violent bid, non-violent commission, and violent bid categories into the violent commission category. There is pressure toward overcoming this situation, a feeling that any outcome whatsoever would be preferable to this. The activity level seems on the point of an exponential leap. Yet the trend is not yet clearly irreversible, the die is not yet cast, the point of no return has not yet been unmistakably reached.

Here we have a classic crisis: *like the crisis point in a severe illness, the outcome may still lie in either direction.*

There is a further possibility. At the point at which the tension from whatever source, including the conditions of uncertainty, becomes sufficiently acute it is likely to tap deeper reservoirs of recollection or stored affect. As these "sunken" perceptions of uncertainty, inadequacy and fear are released, there may take place a sudden surge or flood or explosion of negative affect which will send tension shooting up—to a level which governs both the selection of alternatives and the level of adjustment activity. The outcome is likely to be a change in action category toward violence and a leap of activity level over several orders of magnitude.

NOTES

[1] This appendix is largely derived from Robert C. North and Wilbur Schramm, "International Relations as a Behavioral System."

[2] Ithiel de Sola Pool in "Deterrence As An Influence Process," an unpublished paper, 1962, has pointed out that social science analyses of influence have used two main models that have not been well-reconciled with each other, a stimulus-response, or persuasion model; and the maximizing model used widely by economists. Aspects of both these models are inherent in the present discussion. Like Pool, we believe that the two models are not contradictory; cf. Boulding, *Conflict and Defense,* Chapters 1, 2, 6, 7, and 12.

[3] Cf. Leon Festinger, *A Theory of Cognitive Dissonance* (Evanston and White Plains: Row, Peterson and Co., 1957).

[4] Cf. Morton A. Kaplan, *System and Process in International Politics* (New York: John Wiley and Sons, Inc., 1957), p. 23.

[5] *Ibid.,* pp. 36-43.

[6] Strictly construed, two states in interaction are not coupled, but "non-coupled, corresponding" systems. Cf. Charles E. Osgood and Kellogg V. Wilson, *Some Terms and Associated Measures for Talking About Human Communications* (Urbana: The Institute of Communications Research, 1961). For research purposes, however, it will frequently be convenient to treat non-coupled but corresponding states as if they were coupled.

**PROPOSITIONS FROM
THE 1914 CRISIS**

The Course of the Crisis

The Archduke Francis Ferdinand, heir apparent to the throne of Austria-Hungary, was assassinated June 28, 1914, in the town of Sarajevo by a young Serbian nationalist.

Austria-Hungary perceived the assassination as a threat to itself. As negative affect and tension increased in Vienna, Austro-Hungarian leaders became increasingly concerned with recollections of past threat from Serbia as an outpost of Pan-Slavism. The Austro-Hungarian leaders put forward as a major policy condition the *preservation of the Dual Monarchy at all costs*. Toward this end it was decided to punish Serbia.

Within a week after the assassination Kaiser Wilhelm II of German and his Imperial Chancellor, Dr. von Bethmann-Hollweg, had promised Austria-Hungary what amounted to "blank check" support in an action which was considered likely to eventuate in a localized war against Serbia.

The Austro-Hungarian government presented Serbia with a stern ultimatum on July 23, and five days later the Dual Monarchy declared war against its neighbor.

This Austro-Hungarian adjustment activity (for tension reduction) "snagged," so to speak, with Russia's determination to protect Serbia. More precisely, the Austro-Hungarian decision was perceived by decision-makers in St. Petersburg as threatening an established policy (protection of Serbia) designed to optimize future reward to Russia and minimize punishment by maintaining Slavic solidarity and influence. An attack on Serbia was thus viewed as a threat to Russian security, prestige, and well-being.

On July 29, the day following Austria-Hungary's declaration of war against Serbia, Tsarist Russia—feeling obliged to support a small, fellow-Slav state—ordered, and then cancelled, a general mobilization. It was decided later in St. Petersburg that mobilization would be directed only against Austria-Hungary.

As a consequence of purely technical difficulties the Tsarist government reversed its decision once again on July 30 with a general mobilization—despite German warnings against precipitate hostile actions.

Germany then proclaimed on July 31 a "state of threatening danger of war" and dispatched a twelve-hour ultimatum to Russia which demanded a cessation of preparations on the German frontier.

On the following day, August 1, Germany ordered mobilization and, at 7:00 P.M., declared war on Russia, which had not yet replied to the ultimatum.

Germany, foreseeing a two-front war against Russia to the East and France to the West, tried to secure an initial advantage by invading Luxembourg and presenting Belgium with a demand for permission to cross Belgian territory. This was a state of affairs which Great Britain and France could not tolerate.

Thus, without anyone really intending it, an apparently localized dispute in the Balkans developed into a major European conflict which over succeeding years came to involve a large part of the world.

In a brief six-weeks' span Austria-Hungary's effort to reduce its feeling of threat (by punishing Serbia) had "conflicted" with Russia's determination to protect Serbia. When Russia mobilized (to deter Austria-Hungary), Germany perceived the troop movement as a threat to itself. In an effort to reduce this feeling of threat (perceived as self-protection or self-defense), Germany invoked the Schlieffen Plan, which called for an attack on France through Belgium. For England and France, in turn, the appearance of German troops in Belgium appeared as a threat and thus incited them to reduce the feeling of threat (perceived as self protection or self defense). These perceptions are schematized in Figure A-4.

When the fighting finally ended in 1918, the Austro-Hungarian monarchy had fallen into dissolution and Imperial Germany was on the verge of collapse. By punishing Serbia the

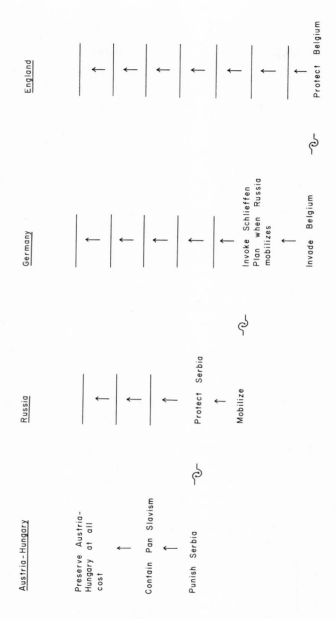

FIGURE A-4

Dual Monarchy, rather than preserve itself, had instituted a chain of events leading to its own downfall. And Germany, which had asserted its intention of maintaining the peace, suffered ignominious defeat in a war for which history was to hold the Kaiser and his colleagues primarily responsible.

In a variety of respects the summer of 1914 presents something close to a classic conflict. One finds here a clearly identifiable period of suspenseful uncertainty. The *pneumococci* of conflict are clearly abroad, but the coping mechanisms of negotiation and other peaceful processes are also operating. Will they be sufficient? Actually, there are two crises: first, a local one; and then a second which escalates from the first.

The local crisis begins with a single transaction of violence. This is followed by negotiations and also by threats of further violence. As the transactional mode of this first crisis becomes increasingly violent—and as the level of violent functioning registers at higher orders of magnitude—the second crisis is set in motion. Now there is a larger outcome in doubt.

The course of these two closely linked crises suggest a series of generalizations for careful testing which one might expect would hold for similar conflicts taking place at other times and in other places, including the present and immediate future. These generalizations pertain to various aspects of state functioning— both domestic and external—and if they should prove valid in a sufficient number of cases one might gain useful insights from them, and also generate, for testing, further, derivative propositions about the ways in which nations behave. Particularly, one might achieve a more precise notion about the behavior of states above a certain level of tension which might be defined as optimal for system functioning.

Domestic Cleavages

Initially, in each of the major capitals, there was outspoken debate about possible alternatives. As the crisis developed, there tended to emerge, broadly speaking, a "war party" and a "peace party,"—though the differences between them were usually matters of emphasis and by no means dichotomous. Increasingly, however, it was the "war party" argument that was heard. In some instances the "peace party" leadership was less and less consulted; in other instances its own attitudes began to change. Altogether, only a small number of persons were involved. Relatively few decision-makers in each capital were aware of the seriousness of the crisis, and even fewer played a significant role in shaping its course. [1]

PREDICTIONS:

The higher the tension (above an optimal level of system functioning)[2], the stronger the tendency on the part of state decision-makers to "suture off" considerable sections of the communications apparatus and to centralize decision-making in the hands of a few top leaders. (Once a decision to go to war has been reached, the tendency is reversed: large numbers of decision-makers are drawn into the effective network.)[3]

The higher the tension, the stronger the tendency for elite perceptions of the crisis to coalesce around a few simplied stereotypes and a limited range of alternatives.

The Austro-Hungarian Empire and the Tsarist Russian Empire were in especially difficult circumstances because of domestic conflicts. Each saw itself internally, as well as externally, threatened, and each was highly conscious of self-preservation as a major purpose.

For decades previous to 1914, Austro-Hungarian leaders had perceived their empire as dangerously threatened by enemies, both domestic and foreign. Among the major dangers, Serbia appeared to stand as an outpost of Pan-Slavism which, under Russian guidance, was seeking to swallow up the Austro-Hungarian Empire. And Slavic minorities, concurrently, were threatening the Dual Monarchy from within. The empire was in danger of losing its position as a "great power." It might even suffer extinction. Any indecision would be interpreted as a weakness.

In Tsarist Russia the lines of cleavage were somewhat different. For large numbers of the population foreign affairs and the prestige of the Russian Empire were far less important than political and economic changes within the system.

In view of the various kinds of dissatisfaction within these two Empires, one might have considered an eruption of internal violence almost as probable as an external war.

PREDICTIONS:

The higher the level of tension within a system, the higher the level of adjustment activity either inside or outside the system—or both—and the higher the probabilities of violence.

A state tends to maintain domestic stability to the degree that its purposes and perceptions are shared by the various component parts of the nation. Generally, the more even the distribution of tension throughout the system, the greater will be the coherence.

When tension associated with a given purpose or perception increases in parts of the system and remains constant or decreases in other parts, a disequilibrium and increasing tendencies toward disruption are likely to appear. The danger is particularly acute if a tension differential exists between the leadership and an important segment of the constituency.

If the tension associated with an operative policy condition is increasingly high among the elite but low among the constituents, the leadership will find it difficult to mobilize the country behind an alternative policy.

If the tension associated with an operative policy condition is low among the elite but increasingly high among the constituents, the system will tend toward disintegration (revolution).

To some degree, at least, the Dual Monarchy hoped to strengthen itself domestically by mobilizing more loyal sectors of the populace against a common enemy. Similarly, the Austro-Hungarian aggression against Serbia provided Tsarist Russia with an external cause which Slavic people in several countries might be expected to champion.

PREDICTION:
If tension is associated by the leadership and the constituency with wholly different perceptions or purposes but is evenly distributed throughout the system, a skillful leadership may be able to manipulate and control tension from all quarters by raising a new perception—especially of common threat—or a new, generally appealing purpose.

In the intermediate run, neither Austro-Hungarian nor Tsarist Russian leaders were shrewd enough or effective enough to contain and manipulate domestic tensions for elite purposes.[4]

Message Volume and Rising Tension

As the crisis developed, decision-makers in the various capitals received rapidly increasing volumes of messages from various parts of Europe. The probability is, however, that as the number of messages increased, fewer of them were read carefully by the decision-makers or briefed for them by their assistants. At the same time, the messages themselves tended to become more and more repetitious and less accurate.

PREDICTIONS:

The higher the tension, the greater the redundancies of communication, the heavier the overload of channels, and the less the ability of decision-makers to assimilate the incoming messages.

The higher the tension, the stronger the tendency for rumor to be transmitted as fact.

With the Austro-Hungarian declaration of war in Serbia the whole tempo of events seemed to quicken, and the various decision-makers began to perceive the environment in new and generally more restricted ways.

PREDICTIONS:

The higher the tension, the "longer" the perception of each time unit and the "shallower" the perception of future time. Each hour will seem an "age," next year will look an "eternity" away, and anything beyond the moment will seem more and more clouded with uncertainity.

The higher the tension, the narrower the range of perceived alternatives and the more restricted the ability to assess the probable consequences of each possible choice.

Except in the very late phases of the crisis, there was relatively little pressure from the public in any of the capitals, nor from the newspapers, to "view with alarm" or to act precipitously. The sense of urgency and of narrowing possibilites of choice were largely generated by the interacting of the decision-makers among themselves.

Perceptions of Fact and Perceptions of Value

The German Empire was subject also to considerable tension, but the sources were different. The nation was not threatened by internal divisiveness; the difficulties emerged from deep feelings of inadequacy and from ambivalences of self-perception and of purpose.

The German perceptual pattern was considerably less consistent than that of the Austro-Hungarians. During the nineteenth century many German leaders, including Bismarck, had been reluctant to acquire colonies or build an empire. Once the nation had embarked on its "new course," however, it pushed forward with mounting enthusiasm and also with uncertainty. Germany was a "great power," but not as great as England. Germany had no quarrel with England, but England was "spreading its net" and seeking world hegemony. Germany was invincible, but it was also "encircled" by hostile forces.

After the turn of the century Germany saw England, France, and Russia closing in from three sides—with Russia seeking also, through a new Balkan Alliance, to close off a fourth side.

By the summer of 1914 Germany was not involved in any serious, overt European conflicts. Indeed, the international arena provided a relatively untroubled appearance. Yet all the perceived uncertainties and threats remained well stored in the memories of the Kaiser and his colleagues and among many influential citizens. On the surface of events they could call for peace and work—up to a point—in order to preserve it. But the

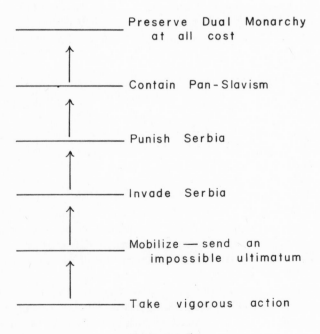

Figure A-5

hostilities were down beneath, ready to erupt if the surface were deeply punctured, ready to flow into a crisis that touched them sufficiently.

During the summer of 1914 Austria-Hungary kept its intentions focused upon waging a war to punish Serbia. Within this frame of reference the Empire's means-end pattern was relatively straightforward—but also single-minded, as indicated by Figure A-5.

Germany, by contrast, tried to play two contradictory roles— that of a Great Power cooperating with other Great Powers to preserve the peace, and that of a faithful ally bound to support Austria-Hungary. Partly Germany acted as a satisfied *status quo* power, and partly, like Austria-Hungary, as a nation threatened and afraid. Thus, we see in Figure A-6 that the German means-end chain was "split down the middle" in that two essentially contradictory courses of action were attempted at the same time.

In the background one finds a close interaction between perceptions of fact and perceptions of choice or preference or decision: each state decides, on the basis of the facts, but each state's perception of fact is partly shaped by the decisions (commitments) it has made or intends to make. Thus, Austria-Hungary and Germany each developed what might be described as a preferred view of the crisis and sought, like Procrustes, to make real fact conform with preferred fact.

According to the Austro-Hungarian preferred view, the invasion of Serbia would be achieved without interference from other states and even with considerable approval. Serbia would be punished and the various threats to the Empire, both internal and external, would be lessened thereby. Austria-Hungary would emerge from the conflict somehow rehabilitated as a great power.

The German preferred view was that Austria-Hungary would succeed in its mission and that Serbia would emerge chastised but "not humiliated." Vienna would make no territorial demands. Russia would object, but not intervene, and England would remain noncommittal. It was doubtful that Austria-Hungary would gain much strength, but the Slavs would be checked, the balance of power preserved, and the principal of monarchy triumphantly upheld. It was conceded that Russian intervention existed as a possibility, but factual perceptions supporting this view were accorded less value than perceptions supporting the opposite possibility.

PREDICTIONS:

The higher the tension, the stronger the tendency to make decisions on the basis of affective feelings rather than cognitive calculations.

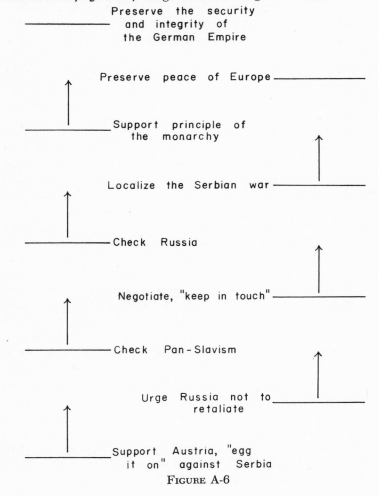

Preserve the security
and integrity of
the German Empire

Preserve peace of Europe

Support principle of
the monarchy

Localize the Serbian war

Check Russia

Negotiate, "keep in touch"

Check Pan-Slavism

Urge Russia not to
retaliate

Support Austria, "egg
it on" against Serbia

FIGURE A-6

The higher the tension, the stronger the tendency for decision-makers to select and interpret incoming messages to reinforce their preconceived views of the crisis.

The higher the tension, the stronger the tendency for a state to perceive another state primarily in terms of whether that state is "with us or against us."[4]

In Berlin and Vienna these selections and adjustments to reinforce the preferred image seem to have been made more or less unconsciously. Among ambassadors in the field, on the other hand, there were opportunities for perceiving "facts" close at hand which tended to challenge the views maintained at the respective centers. A few envoys, notably Prince Lichnowsky, the German Ambassador in London, reported such contradictory information boldly and honestly. Others made adjustments of one sort or another.

In a conversation with Count de Pourtales, the German Ambassador to Russia, for example, the Russian Minister of Foreign Affairs, Sazonov, declared that, "First Serbia was to be eaten up, then it was to be Bulgaria's turn, and then 'we shall have them on the Black Sea.' " In the event that Austria chose to "devour Serbia," Russia would go to war with Austria.

After his conversation with Sazonov, the German Ambassador *noted in his diary* that the Russian Minister of Foreign Affairs had certainly conveyed the impression that the Council of Ministers had "seriously considered the eventuality of a break with Austria-Hungary and Germany" and had decided "not to shrink back from an armed conflict." *In his report to Berlin,* by contrast, the German Ambassador asserted that Sazonov's remark suggested "that it may be concluded that Russia will only take up arms in the event of Austria's attempting to acquire territory at the expense of Serbia." Berlin, of course, had already accepted the "fact" that Austria-Hungary had no intention of seizing territory from Serbia.

Again, as Russia hesitated over mobilization, Pourtales reported back to Berlin his "pleasant impression" that Sazonov's mind had been eased. ". . . Sazonov . . . perhaps as the result of information from Paris and London, has lost some of his nerve and is now looking for a way out."[5]

In Berlin the encouraging word was passed from office to office: Sazonov, the bluffer, was looking for an escape from the crisis.

The higher the tension, the stronger the tendency of agents in the field to report—consciously or unconsciously—that information which they perceive as desired or expected by decision-makers at the center.

Whether Pourtales was fully aware of his own discrepancies is not clear. But Berlin seized upon his estimates, whereas the reports from Prince Lichnowsky were rejected as more non-sense "from that old goat."

There were other ways in which German and Austrian decision-makers tried—consciously or unconsciously—to nudge "facts" into the kind of pattern they preferred to perceive. Since neither Austria-Hungary nor Germany could comfortably contemplate itself as an aggressor, each managed to identify facts placing it in a clearly self-defensive situation. The assassination was a sufficient event to isolate Serbia as an aggressor, but since Serbia was a small nation, it was reassuring for Austria to perceive Russia standing like a puppet master immediately behind.

On July 23 the Austro-Hungarian Government presented Serbia with an ultimatum purposely calculated to evoke rejection, and five days later the Dual Monarchy declared war against its neighbor. As Austro-Hungarian forces began to move, the German Chancellor became increasingly concerned that Vienna should maintain communications with Serbia "in order to prevent a general catastrophe, or at least to put Russia in the wrong . . ."[6]

It is less certain that Germany consciously desired a European war with the intensity that Austria-Hungary wanted an invasion of Serbia. One suspects, however, that much of Berlin's accident prone behavior may have been a response from anxieties and resentments accumulated over the previous quarter century when France and England were riding high and Germany was trying to catch up. It is noteworthy, in any case, how the Kaiser and his colleagues, while calling vociferously for the preservation of peace, by their support of Austria-Hungary, actively precipitated events that made war virtually inevitable.

PREDICTION:

The higher the tension, the stronger the tendency of state A—consciously or unconsciously—either to perceive the crisis in terms which enhance its own self-defensive role; or to make choices which reveal its opponent, B, as deserving of the punishing activity which A is contemplating. Under rising tension State B may be expected to behave similarly.

One is left wondering how often half-hearted negotiation represents the minimum that is considered necessary for defense before the bar of history. And how frequently brinkmanship may constitute an unconscious effort to incite the opponent into intolerable behavior which will fix the blame and render retaliation justifiable.

Perceptions of Capability

Despite the final outcome of the 1914 crisis, it can be argued that—given the information they had available—Austro-Hungarian leaders had every reason to expect some gain to the Empire from the attack on Serbia. The Dual Monarchy had sufficient military capability to subdue Serbia, and no greater power was expected to intervene against Austria-Hungary. Did Imperial Germany have a similar perception of superior capability *vis-a-vis* the larger struggle?

It is widely assumed that a state will not go to war, (that is, commit aggression or allow itself to be drawn into an avoidable war), if it perceives its power (or the power of its coalition) as significantly less than that of the enemy at the time that such a decision must be made. Underlying this hypothesis is the assumption that states commit aggression—or allow themselves to be drawn into an avoidable war—only when they have assessed the consequences as at least minimally favorable. Conversely, a confrontation of superior force, if accurately perceived by the responsible decision-makers, will deter the weaker state from waging an avoidable war.

In fact, for at least two years prior to the assassination, Kaiser

Wilhelm and his advisers had at their disposal evidence of German and Austro-Hungarian military weakness relative to British, Russian, and French capabilities.[7] In spite of this awareness, available Austro-Hungarian and German documents reveal virtually no concern with relative military or industrial capability until the course of events seemed irreversible.

While seeming to disregard their relative lack of capability, German and Austro-Hungarian leaders were not unaware of the catastrophic consequences which might emerge from a major European war. A large-scale conflict was foreseen or a "terrible calamity" and a "holocaust." In a "Summary of the Political Situation" submitted to the Imperial German Chancellor on July 29, the Grand General Staff described the war that might break out as "the mutual butchery of the civilized nations of Europe" which might "annihilate for decades" the civilization of almost the whole continent. In spite of these perceptions, however, the states of Europe continued their march toward war.[8]

PREDICTION:

If a state's perception of injury (or frustration, dissatisfaction, hostility, threat or fear) to itself is "sufficiently" great, this perception will offset perceptions of insufficient capability, making the perception of capability much less important a factor in a decision to go to war.

Rising Tensions and Calculations of Choice

Once troops had begun to move in large numbers, the various threats seemed more imminent and inescapable. Leaders who (probably quite sincerely) had not wanted war began to feel that time had run out, that the enemy was upon them, and that there was no turning back. The German decision-makers were particularly sensitive to a feeling of exposure between perceptions of a hostile Russia already mobilized to the East, a hostile France poised to the West, and a hostile English fleet with steam up ready for action.

From this point forward diplomacy and other coping mechanisms which had constrained the conflict so far became less and less effective.

PREDICTIONS:

The higher the tension, the shorter the time perceived as necessary for the delivery by the enemy of a threatening stimulus.

The shorter the time perceived by a potential target state as required for the delivery of an injurious stimulus of a given magnitude, the greater the perceived threat and the higher the negative affect and consequent tension.

The higher the tension, the stronger the tendency to assess the probable rewards of early action high and the danger of punishment low; concomitantly, the tendency will be to estimate the probable rewards of delay as low and the dangers of punishment as high.

The higher the tension, the stronger the tendency to assess the rewards of violent commissions high (danger of punishment low) and the rewards of non-violent action low (dangers of punishment high).

The higher the tension, the stronger the tendency to assess the rewards of upper levels of system functioning high (probabilities of punishment low) and the rewards of lower levels of system functioning low (probabilities of punishment high).

The higher the tension, the less the ability to seek new solutions for a conflict and the stronger the tendency to choose an alternative habitually associated with the kind of crisis that is perceived.

Rising Tension and the Climax of Crisis

With the Russian mobilization the Kaiser and his colleagues saw their worst fears apparently validated. As long as he had remained convinced that policy-makers in St. Petersburg were bluffing and would not act in defense of Serbia, Wilhelm had performed grandly and confidently as monarch of a powerful empire. During the early morning hours of July 30, however, it became disturbingly evident to officials in Berlin that Russia was mobilizing in earnest. Faced suddenly with what he perceived as an immediate and inescapable threat and with the prospect of what he foresaw as a cataclysmic war, the Kaiser fell back upon a familiar image of a Germany at odds with the world and surrounded by calculating and overpowering enemies. As though he were reaching down toward the bottom of his perceptual reservoir, the Kaiser used symbols that he had not used, hitherto, all summer—words and phrases that had lain like sunken logs in twenty or thirty years of political sediment.

The world, of a sudden, "was plunging headlong" into the "most frightful war" aimed at Germany's downfall. England and France, having laid the foundation of the *casus foederis* by way of Austria, had determined to wage "a war of extermination" against Germany. Thus, by unprincipled calculation and craft Germany had been "brought into a situation" offering England the pretext needed for "annihilating" Germany under the "hypocritical cloak of justice."

The die seemed already cast. Whatever attempts might still be made in search of a peaceful solution appeared scarcely credible. British talk of negotiation and the preservation of peace had been subterfuges to obscure their war-like preparations. Clearly, they could not be trusted.

PREDICTIONS:

At a certain threshold of high tension the value hierarchy of the state is likely to "flip," that is, preferences that were low on the hierarchy move to the top and replace preferences that formerly were considered primary.

The higher the tension, the stronger the tendency to rely upon habitual images and stereotypes.

The higher the tension, the stronger the tendency to interpret a conciliatory move on the part of an opponent state as a trick (or as a sign of weakness, or both).

Out of these threatening events the circumscription of Germany had become a *fact*—in spite of Germany's best efforts to prevent it. "The net has been suddenly thrown over our head," asserted the Kaiser (Bismarck had complained of the "colonial net of England" as early as 1885), "and England sneeringly reaps the brilliant success of her persistently prosecuted purely *anti-German world policy*, against which we have proved ourselves helpless, while she twists the noose of our political and economic destruction out of our fidelity to Austria, as we squirm *isolated* in the net."

PREDICTION:

The higher the tension, the stronger the tendency to accept suspicions and fears as facts.

The Kaiser saw himself and his country outnumbered, out-powered, and trapped by a "hated, lying, conscienceless nation of shopkeepers." Yet Germany would go down fighting neverthe-less. ". . . if we are bled to death," the Kaiser asserted, "England shall at least lose India."

PREDICTION:

The higher the tension, the stronger the tendency to regress toward more elemental modes of behavior.

The resolution of the second, larger crisis of the summer of 1914—*toward war*—seems to have taken place during these early morning hours of July 30. With the abruptly changing percep-tions of Kaiser Wilhelm and others, the coping mechanisms broke down altogether. From this point the conflicts which had been more or less contained by diplomatic procedures became dominant and beyond control. Non-violent bids and commis-sions gave way almost entirely to bids of violence and, increas-ingly over the next few days, to commissions of violence. On an order of magnitude scale, the ensuing violent acts soon registered in the millions—millions of men engaged in violence, millions of resource units consumed, millions of casualties inflicted.

NOTES

[1] See, for example, the Imperial Chancellor to the Ambassador at Vienna, Telegram No. 192, 30 July, 2:55 A.M. *in* Max Montegelas and Walter Schücking (eds.), *Outbreak of the War: German Doc-uments Collected by Karl Kautsky,* translated by the Carnegie En-dowment for International Peace (in one volume), (New York, 1924), No. 395, pp. 444-445 (hereafter referred to as *German Documents,* Kautsky Collection); also Protocol of the Session of the Royal Prussian Ministry of State on July 30, *ibid.,* No. 456, pp. 380-383; and General Staff Memorandum to the Imperial Chancellor, "Summary of the Political Situation," July 29, *ibid.,* No. 348, pp. 306-08.

[2] Unless otherwise stated it will be assumed hereafter that higher levels of tension refer to increments above an hypothetical optimal level for system functioning.

[3] Cf. Richard C. Snyder, *Deterrence, Weapon Systems and Decision-Making.* Studies in Deterrence III, U. S. Naval Ordnance Test Sta-tion, China Lake, California, October 1961, pp. 13, 15-19.

4 To a considerable degree the Marxist-Leninist system which emerged from the chaos of Tsarist disintegration can be viewed as a highly disciplined system for behavior engineering, that is, the impounding of domestic tensions—from whatever source—and the tightly controlled channelling of these tensions to serve the purposes of the governing elite (which are frequently quite different from the purposes of the rank and file).

5 See the report of the German Ambassador dated July 25, *German Documents* (Kautsky Collection) No. **160**, pp. 186-187 and also the communication of the German Ambassador to Bethmann-Hollweg dated July 25, *ibid.*, No. **204**, pp. 213-14. Cf. Graf Friedrich von Pourtalès, *Meine Letzten Verhandlungen in St. Petersburg, Ende Juli 1914* (Berlin: Deutsche Verlagsgesellschaft für Politik und Geschichte, 1927), p. 19; also Luigi Albertini, *The Origins of the War of 1914* (London: Oxford University Press, 1953), Vol. II, p. 301.

6 Germany, Foreign Office, The Imperial Chancellor to the Ambassador at Vienna, Telegram 190, July 30, 1914; 12:30 A.M. Kautsky, No. **384**, p. 339.

7 See memorandum prepared by Ludendorff and signed by von Moltke in December, 1912, General Erich Ludendorff, *The General Staff and Its Problems: The History of the Relations Between the High Command and the German Imperial Government as Revealed by Official Documents*, Vol I, F. A. Holt, trans. (New York, n.d.), p. 64; From the Chief of the General Staff, Colonel General v. Moltke, to the Imperial Chancellor, Dr. v. Bethmann-Hollweg. Germany, Reichsarchiv, *Der Weltkrieg 1947 bis 1918: Kriegsrüstung und Kriegswirtschaft*, Supplement to Vol. I (Berlin, 1930), No. **65**, pp. 192-93; the German Ambassador at St. Petersburg, F. Pourtalès, to the Imperial Chancellor, *German Documents* (Kautsky collection), Nos. **1** and **2**, pp. 53-54; and Ralph Haswell Lutz [ed.], *Fall of the German Empire, 1914-1918*, Vol. II, Hoover War Library Publications, No. 2 (Stanford, 1932), pp. 79-86.

8 The Grand General Staff to the Imperial Chancellor, July 29, 1914. *German Documents* (Kautsky Collection), N. 349, p. 307.

BIBLIOGRAPHY

I. RELEVANT THEORETICAL WORKS

Attneave, Fred. *Applications of Information Theory to Psychology.* New York: Henry Holt and Co., 1959.

Bales, Robert F. *Interaction Process Analysis.* Cambridge, Mass.: Harvard University Press, 1950.

Boulding, Kenneth E. *The Image.* Ann Arbor, Michigan: University of Michigan Press, 1956.

_____. *Conflict and Defense: A General Theory.* New York: Harper and Brothers, 1962.

Cantril, Hadley (ed.), *Tensions That Cause War.* Urbana: University of Illinois Press, 1951.

Coser, Lewis. *Functions of Social Conflict.* Glencoe, Ill.: The Free Press, 1956.

Dollard, John, *et al. Frustration and Aggression.* New Haven, Conn.: Yale University Press, 1939.

Festinger, Leon. *A Theory of Cognitive Dissonance.* Evanston, Ill.: Row, Peterson, 1957.

Hoffmann, Stanley (ed.). *Contemporary Theory in International Relations.* Englewood Cliffs: Prentice-Hall, 1960.

Holsti, Ole R. "The Belief System and National Images: A Case Study," *The Journal of Conflict Resolution,* 6 (1962), 244-252.

Kaplan, Morton A. *System and Process in International Politics.* New York: John Wiley and Sons, Inc., 1957.

Klineberg, Otto. *Tensions Affecting International Understanding: A Survey of Research,* New York: Social Science Research Council, 1950.

Koch, Howard E., North, Robert C., and Zinnes, Dina A. "Some Theoretical Notes on Geography and International Conflict," *The Journal of Conflict Resolution,* 4 (1960), 4-14.

Lasswell, Harold D. *World Politics and Personal Insecurity.* New York: McGraw-Hill, 1935.

Lazarsfeld, Paul (ed.). *Mathematical Thinking in the Social Sciences.* Glencoe, Ill.: The Free Press, 1954.

Lewin, Kurt. *Field Theory in Social Science.* Ed. by Dorwin Cartwright, New York: Harper & Brothers, 1951.

McClelland, Charles A. "Applications of General Systems Theory in International Relations." In James N. Rosenau (ed.), *International Politics and Foreign Policy*. New York: The Free Press of Glencoe, Inc., 1961.

————. "Decisional Opportunity and Political Controversy: The Quemoy Case," *The Journal of Conflict Resolution*, 6 (1962), 201-213.

————. (ed.). *Nuclear Weapons, Missiles, and Future War: Problem for the Sixties*. San Francisco: Howard Chandler, 1960.

————. "The Social Sciences, History, and International Relations." In James N. Rosenau (ed.), *International Politics and Foreign Policy*. New York: The Free Press of Glencoe, Inc., 1961.

Miller, G. A., Galanter, E., and Pribram, K. H. *Plans and the Structure of Human Behavior*. New York: Henry Holt and Co., 1960.

Mowrer, O. H. *Learning Theory and Behavior*. New York: John Wiley & Sons, Inc., 1960.

————. *Learning Theory and the Symbolic Processes*. New York: John Wiley & Sons, Inc., 1960.

North, Robert C., Koch, Howard E., and Zinnes, Dina A. "The Integrative Functions of Conflict," *The Journal of Conflict Resolution*, 4 (1960), 355-374.

Osgood, Charles E. "Behavior Theory and the Social Sciences." In Roland Young (ed.), *Approaches to the Study of Politics*. Evanston: Northwestern University Press, 1958.

————. *Graduated Reciprocation in Tension-Reduction: A Key to Initiative in Foreign Policy*. Urbana: Institute of Communications Research, University of Illinois, December, 1960.

————. "Motivational Dynamics of Language Behavior." In Marshall R. Jones (ed.), *Nebraska Symposium on Motivation*. Lincoln: University of Nebraska Press, 1957.

————. and North, Robert C. "From Individual to Nation: An Attempt to Make Explicit the Usually Implicit Process of Personifying International Relations," an unpublished manuscript. Urbana and Stanford: 1962.

————, and Wilson, Kellogg V. *Some Terms and Associated Measures for Talking About Human Communications*. Urbana: The Institute of Communications Research, 1961.

Rapoport, Anatol. *Fights, Games, and Debates*. Ann Arbor: University of Michigan Press, 1960.

————. "Lewis F. Richardson's Mathematical Theory of War," *The Journal of Conflict Resolution*, 1 (1957), 249-299.

Richardson, Lewis F. *Arms and Insecurity*. Chicago: Quadrangle Books, 1960.

————. *Statistics of Deadly Quarrels*. Chicago: Quadrangle Books, 1960.

Rosenau, James N. (ed.), *International Politics and Foreign Policy: A Reader in Research and Theory*. New York: The Free Press of Glencoe, Inc., 1961.

Schelling, Thomas C. *The Strategy of Conflict*. Cambridge, Mass.: Harvard University Press, 1960.

Skinner, B. F. *Science and Human Behavior*. New York: Macmillan, 1953.

————. *Verbal Behavior*. New York: Appleton-Century-Crofts, 1957.

Snyder, Richard C., Bruck, H. W., and Sapin, Burton. *Decision-Making as an Approach to the Study of International Politics*. Princeton: Organizational Behavior Section, Princeton University, June, 1954. Reprinted in the same authors' *Foreign Policy Decision-Making*. New York: The Free Press of Glencoe, Inc., 1962, pp. 14-185.

————, and Robinson, James A. *National and Internatinoal Decision-Making*. New York: Institute for International Order, 1961.

Wasserman, Paul, and Silander, Fred S. *Decision-Making: An Annotated Bibliography*. Ithaca, N.Y.: 1958.

Wiener, Norbert. *Cybernetics*. New York: Wiley, 1948.

Wright, Quincy. "Design for a Research Proposal on International Conflict and the Factors Causing Their Aggravation or Amelioration," *Western Political Science Quarterly*, 10 (1957), 263-275.

————. *The Study of Internatoinal Relations*. New York: Appleton-Century-Crofts, Inc., 1955.

————. *The Study of War*. Chicago: University of Chicago Press, 2 vol., 1942.

Zinnes, Dina A., North, Robert C., and Koch, Howard E. "Capability, Threat, and the Outbreak of War." In James N. Rosenau (ed.), *International Politics and Foreign Policy*. New York: The Free Press of Glencoe, Inc., 1961.

————. "Hostility in International Decision-Making," *The Journal of Conflict Resolution*, 6 (1962), 236-243.

II. DATA COLLECTION AND PROCESSING

Berelson, Bernard. "Content Analysis." In Gardner Lindzey (ed.), *Handbook of Social Psychology*. Cambridge, Mass.: Addison-Wesley, 1954, pp. 488-522.

————. *Content Analysis in Communications Research*. Glencoe: The Free Press, 1952.

Block, Jack. *The Q-Sort Method in Personality Assessment and Psychiatric Research*. Springfield, Ill.: Charles C Thomas, 1961.

Cartwright, Dorwin P. "Analysis of Qualitative Material." In Leon Festinger and Daniel Katz (eds.), *Research Methods in the Behavioral Sciences*. New York: Dryden Press, 1953, pp. 421-70.

Dollard, John, and Mowrer, O. H. "A Method of Measuring Tension in Written Documents," *Journal of Abnormal and Social Psychology*, 42 (1947), 1-32.

George, Alexander L. *Propaganda Analysis: A Study of Inferences Made From Nazi Propaganda in World War II.* Evanston, Ill.: Row, Peterson, 1959.

Haas, Michael. "Thematic Content Analysis in the Study of Diplomatic Documents," Studies in International Conflict and Integration, Stanford University (dittoed), August 15, 1961.

Janis, Irving L. "Meaning and the Study of Symbolic Behavior," *Psychiatry,* 6 (1943), 425-39.

Lasswell, Harold D., Lerner, Daniel, and Pool, Ithiel de Sola. *The Comparative Study of Symbols.* Stanford: Stanford University Press, 1952.

_____, and Blumenstock, Dorothy. *World Revolutionary Propaganda.* New York: A. A. Knopf, 1939.

_____, Leites, Nathan, et al. *Language of Politics: Studies in Quantitative Semantics.* New York: George W. Stewart, 1949.

_____. *Propaganda Technique in the World War.* New York: A. A. Knopf, 1927.

_____. "The World Attention Survey," *Public Opinion Quarterly,* 5 (1941), 456-62.

Lazarsfeld, Paul F., and Barton, Allen H. "Qualitative Measurement in the Social Sciences: Classification, Typologies, and Indices." In Daniel Lerner, Harold D. Lasswell (eds.), *The Policy Sciences: Recent Development in Scope and Method.* Stanford: Stanford University Press, 1951.

Lerner, Daniel, and Lasswell, Harold D. (eds.). *The Policy Sciences: Recent Developments in Scope and Method.* Stanford: Stanford University Press, 1951.

McNemar, Quinn. *Psychological Statistics.* Second edition, New York: John Wiley & Sons, Inc., 1955.

North, Robert C. "International Conflict and Integration: Problems of Research." In Muzafer Sherif (ed.), *Intergroup Relations and Leadership.* New York: John Wiley & Sons, 1962.

Osgood, Charles E., Saporta, Sol, and Nunnally, Jim C. "Evaluative Assertion Analysis," *Litera,* 3 (1956), 47-102.

_____, Suci, George J., and Tannenbaum, Percy H. *The Measurement of Meaning.* Urbana: University of Illinois Press, 1957.

_____, and Walker, Evelyn G. "Motivation and Language Behavior: A Content Analysis of Suicide Notes," *Journal of Abnormal and Social Psychology,* 59 (1959), 58-67.

Peak, Helen. "Problems of Objective Observation." In Leon Festinger and Daniel Katz (eds.), *Research Methods in the Behavioral Sciences.* New York: The Dryden Press, 1953.

Pool, Ithiel de Sola. *Symbols of Internationalism.* Stanford: Stanford University Press, 1951.

————, (ed.), *Trends in Content Analysis*. Urbana: University of Illinois Press, 1959.

Robinson, James A. "Further Problems of Research on International Relations." In Muzafer Sherif (ed.), *Intergroup Relations and Leadership*. New York: John Wiley & Sons, 1962.

Robinson, W. S. "The Statistical Measurement of Agreement," *American Sociological Review*, 22 (1957), 17-25.

Schutz, William C. "On Categorizing Qualitative Data in Content Analysis," *Public Opinion Quarterly*, 22 (1958-59), 503-15.

————. "Reliability, Ambiguity and Content Analysis," *Psychological Review*, 59 (1952), 119-29.

Scott, William A. "Reliability of Content Analysis: The Case of Nominal Scale Coding," *Public Opinion Quarterly*, 19 (1955), 321-25.

Siegel, S. *Non-Parametric Statistics for the Behavioral Sciences*. New York: McGraw Hill, 1956.

Stephenson, William. *The Study of Behavior: Q-Technique and Its Methodology*. Chicago: The University of Chicago Press, 1953.

White, Ralph K. *Value Analysis, the Nature and Use of the Method*. Glen Gardner, New Jersey: Society for the Psychological Study of Social Issues, 1951.

III. TECHNIQUES OF ANALYSIS

Borko, Harold (ed.), *Computer Applications in the Behavioral Sciences*. Englewood Cliffs: Prentice-Hall, 1962.

Fruchter, Benjamin. *Introduction to Factor Analysis*. Princeton, N.J.: D. Van Nostrand Co., Inc., 1954.

Guetzkow, Harold, Alger, Chadwick F., Noel, Robert, and Brody, Richard A. *The Use of Simulation for Research and Teaching in International Relations*. Englewood Cliffs: Prentice-Hall, 1963.

Harman, Henry A. *Modern Factor Analysis*. Chicago: University of Chicago Press, 1960.

Hays, D. G. "Automatic Content Analysis Analysis: Some Entries for a Transformation Catalogue," Santa Monica: The RAND Corporation, 1960.

Locke, William N. "Translation by Machine," *Scientific American* (January, 1956), 20-33.

The Research Laboratory of Electronics and the Computation Center. *An Introduction to COMIT Programming*. Cambridge, Mass.: M.I.T., 1961.

————. COMIT Programmer's Reference Manual. Cambridge: Mass.: M.I.T., 1961.

Snyder, Richard C. "Game Theory and the Analysis of Political Behavior." In James N. Rosenau (ed.), *International Politics and Foreign Policy*. New York: The Free Press of Glencoe, Inc., 1961.

Stone, Philip J., Bales, Robert F., Namenwirth, J. Zvi, and **Ogilvie**,

Daniel M. "The General Inquirer: A Computer System for Content Analysis and Retrieval Based on the Sentence as a Unit of Information," *Behavioral Science,* 7 (1962), 484-494.

Wright, Quincy. "Measurement of Variations in International Tensions." In Bryson, Finkelstein, and MacIver (eds.), *Learning and World Peace,* Eighth Symposium on Science, Philosophy and Religion, New York: Harper, 1948, 54 ff.

Yngve, Victor H. "COMIT as an IR Language," *Communications of the Association for Computing Machinery* (January 1962), 19-26.

_____. "Computer Program for Translation," *Scientific American* (June 1962), 68-76.

Zaninovich, M. George. "Pattern Analysis of Variables Within the International System: The Sino-Soviet Example," *The Journal of Conflict Resolution,* 6 (1962), 253-68.